The
INTELLIGENT
GUIDE
to the 6TH
SENSE

The
INTELLIGENT
GUIDE
to the 6TH
SENSE

HEIDI SAWYER

HAY HOUSE

Australia • Canada • Hong Kong • India
South Africa • United Kingdom • United States

Please Note: This book was previously published as *Why My Mother Didn't Want Me to Be a Psychic*. All material is unchanged from the previous edition.

First published and distributed in the United Kingdom by:
Hay House UK Ltd, 292B Kensal Rd, London W10 5BE.
Tel.: (44) 20 8962 1230; Fax: (44) 20 8962 1239. www.hayhouse.co.uk

Published and distributed in the United States of America by:
Hay House, Inc., PO Box 5100, Carlsbad, CA 92018-5100. Tel.: (1) 760 431 7695
or (800) 654 5126; Fax: (1) 760 431 6948 or (800) 650 5115. www.hayhouse.com

Published and distributed in Australia by:
Hay House Australia Ltd, 18/36 Ralph St, Alexandria NSW 2015.
Tel.: (61) 2 9669 4299; Fax: (61) 2 9669 4144. www.hayhouse.com.au

Published and distributed in the Republic of South Africa by:
Hay House SA (Pty), Ltd, PO Box 990, Witkoppen 2068. Tel./Fax: (27) 11 467 8904.
www.hayhouse.co.za

Published and distributed in India by:
Hay House Publishers India, Muskaan Complex, Plot No.3, B-2, Vasant Kunj,
New Delhi – 110 070. Tel.: (91) 11 4176 1620; Fax: (91) 11 4176 1630.
www.hayhouse.co.in

Distributed in Canada by:
Raincoast, 9050 Shaughnessy St, Vancouver, BC V6P 6E5.
Tel.: (1) 604 323 7100; Fax: (1) 604 323 2600

The author of this book does not dispense medical advice or prescribe the use of any
technique as a form of treatment for physical or medical problems without the advice of
a physician, either directly or indirectly. The intent of the author is only to offer information of a general nature to help you in your quest for emotional and spiritual wellbeing.
In the event you use any of the information in this book for yourself, which is your con-
stitutional right, the author and the publisher assume no responsibility for your actions.

A catalogue record for this book is available from the British Library.

ISBN 978-1-84850-224-6

Printed and bound in the UK by CPI Bookmarque, Croydon, CR0 4TD.

Dedication
To the misunderstood

About the Author

Heidi Sawyer is a British psychic, healer, writer and course facilitator. She travels the UK and abroad teaching psychic awareness, self-healing and hands-on healing, including her very popular Mahutmu Healing techniques.

Heidi has written numerous articles on psychic development, and her very popular home psychic-development courses are sold around the world. Her course material is regularly used for research in radio and television programmes about psychic abilities.

For details on Heidi's courses, workshops and home psychic development, or to sign up to her free psychic development monthly newsletter that includes tips and information, please visit www.PsychicCourses.com.

'It amazes me how someone can explain such a seemingly complex subject in a way that even I can understand!'
Judy Pinner, mum

'The powerful stories, analogies and facts contained within this book have had no less than a profound impact on my life. Thank you!'
John Milton, sales manager

'The famous Buddhist insight, "Before enlightenment, chop wood, carry water; after enlightenment, chop wood, carry water," springs into mind as I have had the same feeling following reading Heidi's book! My world is the same, yet I look at everything in it so differently.'
Laura Benson, secretary

' "When the student is ready the teacher will appear." This is certainly what happened to me. When I was ready, I met Heidi. I wish you my kind of good fortune!'
Linda Penny, complementary health practitioner

'I loved the chapter on Psychic Children because, clearly being the parent of one, it is a pleasant change to finally meet someone who understands what it is like, rather than someone who tries to label my son as having ADHD or some other awfully corrosive thought.'
Katherine Williamson, mum

'I have picked up a countless number of what Heidi calls "energy lanterns" whilst reading this book, but far more importantly I now know how to observe the "energy stealers" in my life and that it is OK. I now know what I can do about it.'
Tessa McCallian, human resources manager

'Are you what Heidi calls a "soaring eagle", or are you stuck thinking you are a "pigeon"? We are all eagles; some of us simply don't know it yet. This book will help you find out how.'
Alexandra McLean-Williams, theatrical agent

'Are you, like me, fascinated with bright colours such as pink, purple and white? Having read this book, I now know what this means: I am not weird, mentally unwell or anything else I have been called by my close friends and family, but most importantly for me I also know I am not alone.'
Jennifer Fratton, administrator

'Heidi's three-stage "Opening Process" was amazing. It was like someone was writing about me and my experiences!'
Nevil Parker, systems analyst

'The stories in this book are so profound and meaningful, and the analogies are so self-explanatory, that I only wish I had discovered Heidi's material sooner.'
Henry Roker, tree surgeon

'A close friend of mine recommended this book to me; she was a little coy about it because we had never discussed anything quite like this before, even as friends. Now, however, we can't stop talking about it!'
Katie Friary, personal assistant

'Although Heidi is clearly very skilled and has been training for years, she gives me the impression that with her help I, too, can achieve what she can do in a fraction of the time. In fact, by simply following a couple of the suggestions in this book I have already had psychic experiences of my very own!'
Rosemary Cummings, retired midwife

'I love how she says, "You don't find many accountants who have to justify their competence with numbers when they meet a client for the first time, so why do psychics have to tell someone the colour of that person's underwear in order to be believed?" It is time to move beyond this naiveté and respect those in this field because I believe they are an integral part of our understanding on spirituality.'
Graham McAllister, accountant

CONTENTS

Acknowledgements

First I would like to thank my mother. Her beliefs were the inspiration to write this book, and her continued dedication to helping me with childcare made it possible to get this work published. I would also like to thank my father, and I appreciate my husband for remaining awake with me until two o'clock in the morning while I wrote it. Last but not least, I would like to thank my sister Kimberly for her never-ending belief and loyalty.

FOREWORD

We all have questions about the mysterious, the miraculous, the inexplicable and seemingly impossible phenomena that occur in our lives. They come at various stages in life, sometimes gradually and sometimes 'out of the blue', when one is faced with events that fall out of harmony with our everyday experiences. Often, such happenings can prompt the big life questions of existence and purpose. We all must face the questions of our existence, the 'Why am I here? Where did I come from? Where do I go when I die?' questions. We also often question the purpose of our existence, wondering, 'Why is this happening? What does it mean? Why me?' Sometimes those questions simply will not cease being asked; as the poet Emily Dickinson once wrote, they are like teeth that 'nibble at the soul', refusing to let go of one's psyche. What do we do with them? How do we answer them? How do we deal with them?

Indeed, we all must face these questions, and each one of us will respond uniquely. Yet when we begin to explore them, when we begin to take notice of what is happening in and around us, we begin to notice that we are not alone with these questions. After all, we do not live in isolation! Instead, there are histories of people we begin to come into contact with who have the same questions that we do! Chances are that you are one such person: someone who has been prompted to search deeper and to explore, someone for whom the mundane is not enough, someone who simply *has* to know more. I, too, am one such person. From early in my life I began to ponder the nature of existence and its purpose. I was beset with curiosities about a life beyond this one. As a result I have been blessed with myriad fantastic experiences and meetings with remarkable people to whom I have listened, with whom I have engaged in various ways, with whom I have talked and shared, and from whom I have learned and continue to learn. It is difficult to articulate how grateful I am for those questions and the individuals around me who sought to help me answer them!

Heidi Sawyer is one such remarkable person; indeed, she is truly remarkable! Having heard about her work, I had the privilege of meeting Heidi, thanks to an introduction from a respected friend and colleague who told me that we simply *had* to meet. We 'met' first on the telephone. It was one of those 'meetings' that brought an immediate sense of familiarity, of intimacy and of respect, even though we 'met' only through our voices transmitted over the ether. Nevertheless, our telephone calls led us to the immediate conclusion that we had to meet in person. Intuitively, instinctively and psychically I knew that this would be a life-changing meeting, one that would lead to developments and consequences that would affect not only both of our lives but also the lives of countless others.

When we met in one of my consulting rooms at The Diagnostic Clinic in New Cavendish Street, London, my initial impression was immediately confirmed. I found myself in the presence of an unusually gifted, intelligent and powerful woman committed to living an authentic life; her forthright honesty and courage immediately became evident. Heidi's journey through disease to deepening health and wholeness has brought her through great suffering of all types: physical, emotional, intellectual and spiritual. As we began to explore our respective situations, it was clear to both of us that the next steps demanded nothing less than total commitment. The work that Heidi describes in this book, her life's work thus far, is all about that commitment. This is no work of theory or fancy intellectualism. This is the outcome of a life of dedication, of long training, practice and deep inner resolve. It is the fruit of a vine that has been meticulously and very carefully pruned and nurtured.

I have worked as a physician, scientist, journal editor, academic and healer for over 30 years. Since early childhood I have been interested in the 'magical' and in mystery, utterly fascinated by the transformation of one thing into another, such as the metamorphosis of the caterpillar into the butterfly. I was keenly aware of the healing effects of my mother's hands that could become so very hot and made me feel so wonderfully different when she touched me if I was ill. I have always been acutely sensitive to the fact that some people could 'touch' me and 'knew' so much more about me than could have been known by ordinary means. I knew whilst at school that biomedical science could not provide me with the answers I was seeking. Nevertheless, I knew I needed to understand its language in order to function and progress in my understanding and to bridge the worlds I had met: the numinous, which Rudolf Otto used to describe those 'wholly other' invisible worlds, and the material world, the visible, physical world of everyday experience. The apprenticeship in science during my tenure as a medical student restricted my exploration of the psychic and healing realms, but the incessant search to keep those faculties alive never died. I nurtured them, stored up the experiences and determined that I would bring them all together, determining ultimately to utilize them in serving others. Heidi's book is a brilliant guidebook for those seeking to do the same, to explore what it means to identify, understand, use and develop those skills. Her work is the instruction manual needed not only to begin that work but also to develop it.

In my own work as a consultant physician and medical homeopath in integrative medicine and healthcare and in Jungian analytical psychology and healing, I have encountered many people with great wisdom, knowledge and understanding, alongside charlatans and impostors claiming psychic abilities, healing gifts and mystical knowledge. Yes, the world of healing is a professional minefield! Amongst them all, Heidi Sawyer is a gem, a genuine soul of great integrity. Her book is a direct, down-to-earth, practical and no-nonsense resource, clearly written to assist and support individual and collective healing. It is a book that shows that there *is* a science to this work, there *are* roadmaps, and that there *is* structure that conforms to law. If followed, her guidance will help those seeking to find their way and to come to their senses, especially the sixth! This material may be centuries old, but it is no less relevant now than it was in the farthest reaches of antiquity. Even if she were only describing the terrain and the range of phenomena that there are to be encountered in the field, this book would render great service.

However, Heidi does much more in this book. She brings together an atlas of the terrain alongside a detailed roadmap and instruction manual warning of pitfalls and alerting the reader to watering holes and hidden opportunities that might not otherwise be visible. In so doing, she renders a service which will evoke gratitude in many hearts and minds, especially at this time when so many are awakening to their gifts and seeking to understand how to use and nurture them. In each chapter there is clear, concise material describing what may be felt or experienced, what can be done and what to look out for as one progresses through different stages in the evolution of the psyche. In this, it is an invaluable resource. Enjoy the book, learn from it and savour it. Read it from cover to cover or dip into it, knowing that what will serve in that moment will be offered in the pages on which the book falls open!

Professor Kim A. Jobst, MA, DM, MRCP, MFHom, DipAc
September 2008

INTRODUCTION

Whether at school, college, university or work, when I was tuned in to my sixth sense and operating by it, the results I gained were phenomenal. The moment I slipped into my 'ego' self, I lost confidence and results. Everybody has a sixth sense, but many of us either don't know it or we choose to ignore it. Psychic development is the earliest part of very deep and profound change in our inner world, for it is the process of getting to know yourself. If you are like me, you will want a quick route that is pain-free with lasting results.

At the beginning of becoming aware of intuitive and psychic abilities, I remember some key questions I certainly had. The key questions over the years have not changed, and I still get asked them on a daily basis:

- How do you know if you're psychic?
- I've had some strange experiences I don't understand; can you explain them for me?
- How do I explore my psychic side?
- What does it mean to be psychic?
- How do you deal with it?
- Who is it that stands at the bottom of my bed, and how do I get them to go away?

This book is the product of my journey so far, both from years of teaching people psychic awareness and as a result of my own personal process from rejection to acceptance. It explores the opening to the inner self. By the time you have finished it, you will have an excellent understanding of your sixth sense and how to use it for your best interests. Psychic ability enables us to 'tune in' to the energies around us; understanding it is the key to experiencing what it provides. But be advised: psychic skills are not party tricks, and opening yourself to this side of you creates huge potential within your awareness and sensitivity.

This book is designed for you to either read from cover to cover or dip into as a reference. With stories interspersed, it will spark your interest in the deeper, more spiritual side of your nature.

CHAPTER 1

The Opening – Beginning of Natural Psychic Skills

'Those who have developed "psychic" powers have simply let some of the limitations they laid upon their minds be lifted.'
A Course in Miracles

I remember clearly the first time I knew I had experienced the spirit world. Reversing out of the driveway on my way to the supermarket, a figure caught my eye. It darted from the front room, appearing to be dressed all in black. I sat frightened in the car, thinking a burglar had waited until I had left the house before moving from his hiding place.

Continuing to look, I thought to myself, 'Burglars do not pass through walls and remain standing looking at you.' The figure moved closer to the front door, and as it did I saw a very happy woman, approximately in her seventies, waving at me. It was my grandmother who had passed over into spirit a few years previously. Relieved it wasn't a burglar, I continued on my way to the supermarket. From that point forward for the next few months, I wandered around very confused. I had no way of understanding what had happened. No one in my immediate surroundings understood what I had experienced. Most thought I had temporarily lost my mind or they didn't want to discuss it, as such things frightened them.

Like me with my first experience, most people fear the unknown, and anything out of the ordinary often fills them with anguish. Most of us are brought up with linear, logical thinking, and our spiritual and psychic side is often squashed in early childhood as part of a vivid imagination. We forget we have these amazing skills that we naturally possess, so we stuff them deep down into the place where no one goes until a chipping starts and the flame of the light-worker within ignites, and a stretch for development begins. For many, this reveals itself through constant and prolific flashes of intuition, the strong desire to change and grow, the fascination with bright colours such as pink, purple and white, or the meeting of spirits (as in my experience) or hearing their name being called when no one else is in the room.

Some of these things start with strong changes in your life, or perhaps they follow emotional trauma. Psychologists and psychiatrists have a less than polite name for it, but I have noticed a recurring pattern in a lot of people during my many years of teaching psychic development. What I call 'the Opening' starts in similar ways for most people.

Stage One Opening – Common Signs

- coincidences occurring in your life
- seeing things out of the corner of your eye
- feeling a 'breeze' or a presence
- strong fascination for psychic or spiritual knowledge
- receiving 'messages' in dreams from friends or relatives who have died
- dreaming of events before they happen
- seeing those who are no longer alive

- hearing things repeated over and over in your mind
- people wanting to tell you their life history and things they have rarely told others, even if they do not know you very well
- 'knowing' people well when you have only met them recently
- strong feelings regarding the health of others which you later find out were correct
- sensitivity to noise
- sensitivity to the moods of others
- sudden and strong desires to clean up your health and eating habits
- fascination with angels or fairies
- being inexplicably drawn to the colours lilac, pink or white
- rubbing your forehead often and wanting to get hair away from your face. Strange pulling sensation across the forehead ('third eye' stretching)
- wanting to 'save' others and the planet

Downside to Stage One Opening

- increased irritability
- intolerance where previously you have been very tolerant
- willingness to speak up when previously you have kept quiet
- temporarily unreliable

Stage One Opening provides a grounding basis from which to work. Many who experience Stage One do so for quite some time before they decide to investigate and move further. Stage One can accompany fear and significant change in a person's life. This is because the drive of the inner world and spiritual shifts can conflict with the personality and cause fear within the ego. The ego is the part of you that makes decisions based on the self and perhaps on logical thinking, rather than the 'gut' feelings that so often tell the truth, even though this truth can be uncomfortable or the temptation can be to resist change.

The real issue with ignoring Stage One Opening can be the increase in activity from spirit and from your psychic channels; this will not go away and will only increase as you get older. As you are opening up and have a strong sensitivity to the psychic or intuitive side, you may find that life seems to conspire against you. It is not because some evil spirit is waiting to clonk you one; rather, it is because a part of you which wants to expand and change physically, emotionally and spiritually is being pushed back in every time it tries to escape. Fear will try to repress your psychic growth. You may experience fear of the unknown, fear of change and fear of growth because your psychic self creates change you can't control. The good news is, once Stage One is embraced wholeheartedly in a trusting manner, interference from spirit will settle down and, if need be, go away to allow the continuation of the Opening at your own pace.

One woman I have observed over the years was desperately trying to avoid Stage One Opening. She would keep herself overly busy with work and with trotting from one failed relationship to another. For this particular woman, opening to her psychic and intuitive side was about self-esteem. Once she embraced this part of herself and started to develop it, she realized that her relationships hadn't worked because she was going through intense and constant inner change. Once it all began to settle down, she met a man with whom she is very happy and has been for several years. She let herself slow down enough to realize that by accepting her instincts she made brave moves to new territory

4

that seemed to happen very naturally. The visits from spirit that she had once been disturbed by settled down, and she began to pass on very helpful insights to her friends and family, whereas previously she had been frightened of 'bad' things happening.

Stage Two Opening

- suddenly feeling you are uncomfortable in this world and wanting to go 'home', although it is unclear where 'home' is
- releasing strong emotions through unexplainable tears
- intolerance to alcohol
- increase in allergies
- strong desire for periods of silence and solitude
- strong desire to find 'purpose'
- requiring deep relationships and a desire to move away from what you increasingly find superficial
- deep feeling within that change is about to happen, but can't put your finger on it
- feeling you want to do something that significantly helps others

Downside to Stage Two Opening

- wanting to 'help' everyone
- 'Messiah complex' or feeling you are 'the chosen one', so to speak, and that your healing technique or choices are better than others. This is often a temporary phase and a reaction to an increase in energy flow.
- reluctance to indulge in over-eating or drinking – this can be seen by friends and family as being anti-social

- feeling less connected to friends, relationships and family dynamics. This can feel as though your friends are disappearing from your life or you have little still in common because you have 'changed'. Again, this is a temporary situation and a reaction to energy shifts.

Stage Two Opening for some people corresponds to and happens simultaneously with Stage One. Stage Two can, on the one hand, be completely calming; on the other, it can be very alarming. Stage Two Opening allows for a deeper connection to your inner worlds and a knowledge of what is truly important to you. Intense flashes of intuition allow for profound and memorable changes to occur. These may take the form of complete external changes in your life – a career change, house move, new relationship, often all at the same time. These tend to occur when a part of your life isn't progressing along a destined path and you need a bit of encouragement to get there. The more alarming part of this stage, which happens for some people but not all, is the 'clearing' process that tends to occur with it. This is a bit of clearing out of the unnecessary parts of your life, the parts that will deplete you of your energies, and it is an essential (if uncomfortable) part of your psychic development.

The strong feeling of not belonging in this world and wanting to 'go home' can be quite intense for some people. When this occurs, you know that a person is going through an amazing shift in consciousness and that their psyche has begun to trust in a part of life larger than their personality. Fortunately, crying for no real reason does not usually accompany depressed feelings. If it does, the depressed feelings are very temporary. There is a strong distinction between an Opening and clinical depression. An Opening does not display typical depression symptoms. Instead, a Stage Two Opening will only manifest short-term emotional releases, accompanied by intense feelings leaving the body.

A chap who came to see me on several occasions was having typical Stage Two Opening symptoms. As many Stage-Two individuals do, he wanted to make changes in his life and work. He wanted to help people and he wanted to find his sense of purpose. These longings were corresponding with Stage One Opening symptoms, such as increased activity from spirit, pushing hair away from his face and a constant pulling feeling across his forehead. I started some healing work with this man and began to channel a level of energy that was appropriate to what his body seemed to request. Before long his body began to twist and turn and a strong choking noise came from his throat. As the healing continued I could see a grey mist begin to appear and then clear around his throat and head area. With that, he began to sob uncontrollably. The poor man was deeply embarrassed, as he had not cried in 30 years and couldn't understand where it was coming from or what it was about. After a few minutes the crying stopped and he felt fine. He said his body felt very light, and off he went.

The next time I saw him he reported how his life had very suddenly shifted and changed. He explained how he had actively embraced the changes and his skills, and that his confidence and ability within his working environment had increased to the extent that he had received a promotion to a very senior position within one of the world's largest companies. He was helping people within this environment create the best within themselves. He continues to acknowledge the psychic and highly intuitive part of his nature by responding wholeheartedly when this part of himself makes itself known or wants him to respond to events in life that perhaps others would be deeply afraid of.

The downside of Stage Two Opening can be, for some people, an area they need to watch closely. This is particularly the case if you have had a profound spiritual or psychic experience and want to shout about it from the rooftops. It is often best to keep these things to yourself or to choose carefully with whom you share them. People going through Stage Two often want to 'fix' everyone, or they believe their method of healing or development is the *only* route rather than *a* route. For most, this is a temporary situation and settles down after a while.

Likewise, for others, an emerging 'Messiah complex' can be a little alarming. This will mean they believe themselves to be part of a second coming, and this can be accompanied with strong new psychic skills. People with 'Messiah complex' type symptoms, as has been my observation, do display some of the energies associated with the Ascended Masters, but they are in fact only drawing on these energies. It is the personality or ego self that is often identifying with the idea that they are a reincarnation of Christ or Mary Magdalene, and often accompanies a period of low self-esteem. It may be coincidental, but the people I have come across going through this particular part of Stage Two tend to be going through relationship troubles.

Stage Three Opening

- strong connection to intuition and instinct
- trust of intuition and instinct
- growing sense of fearlessness (will do what you want to do even if scared)
- strong commitment to self-growth, whatever the consequences
- disappearance of addictive traits, such as drinking too much alcohol and smoking

- strong self-discipline
- emergence of committed and strong relationships in life.
- speaking the truth kindly
- feeling a 'jarring' in energy field if unkind words are spoken
- increased feeling of neutrality where strong feelings have been present previously, e.g. in cases of hostility, fear, mistrust
- seeing people for who they are and not expecting them to change to suit your needs
- willing and able to leave situations that no longer work for you
- dissolving of abandonment fears. Comfortable in your own company, not fearful of people leaving you. May prefer being alone.
- very strong sensitivity to the energy fields of others
- clear and accurate interpretations of the emotional states of others, free of judgement and fear
- consistency in emotional levels. No extreme highs or lows.
- people comment on how everything goes your way
- considered lucky
- considered wise
- great trust in the process
- easily able to 'let go' of things, people, feelings and situations, especially negative ones
- learn from life challenges; easily able to drop resentments
- able to spot and willing to change negative thought patterns
- strongly improved self-image
- no longer need to 'save' others but make a significant contribution to the development of others (don't need to shout about it)

- make a conscious effort to prolong and enhance the life of the planet by contributing to energy-saving methods, but no longer need to 'save' it single-handedly

- no fear of 'darkness', awareness that it is simply a lack of light

- terrific insight into the unconscious motivations of others, requiring little effort

- drive is for continued self-expression rather than to prove anything

Downside to Stage Three Opening

People experiencing a Stage Three Opening can be seen as cold and uncaring. This is not the case, since people experiencing this level are not often in denial of anything that might create a need to shut out their feelings. People around someone going through this stage may not like the way that person does not react to their ideas, or acknowledge their attempts at manipulation. Furthermore, displaying a lack of guilt means that others find it difficult to incite a sense of duty from someone going through this stage; therefore, hostility from others in the early part of this stage may seem prolific as people adjust to your new behaviours.

The above stages are merely my observations from teaching psychic development since 1996. Some of the stages will cross into others; hence, you may have experienced some, but not all, of the aspects of the various stages. However, those who have reached Stage Three Opening experiences will have a fairly concise and consistent list. None of the stages is better than the others; each is simply an extension of the one that precedes it. Certainly those entering Stage Three have lost the sense of 'ego' and operate from a confident place within the self. This is not to say they are perfect. They do tend to show many of the downside traits on a regular basis, which may lead to a short-term mini-crisis, especially in the opinion of loved ones who are not familiar with the 'new' person.

Nevertheless, people experiencing Stage Three Opening are showing very visible evidence of positive changes in their interactions with others. Therefore, it is important to emphasize that although these 'opening stages' can at first appear frightening, in my experience they will increase until you have acknowledged and developed the intuitive aspect of the self. Once this aspect is embraced, many of the negative side effects will settle down.

To return to my own story, following the vision of my grandmother which I had experienced, I tried to forget about it. To my detriment I found my experience of the activity in the house increased dramatically. On many occasions I could feel her presence, I could smell the cigarettes she smoked, and I heard my name being called loudly. This, for me, was not within my head, but appeared from a stern female voice trying to attract my attention. It seemed as though someone was standing right next to me, but no one was physically there. I also heard a very loud knocking, as though someone was rapping her knuckles on the windowsill. Still, I tried to ignore these experiences.

When it became too much and I was frightened, I finally told my mother. After all, it was in my parents' house that I was experiencing the phenomena. This was at a time when psychic experiences were not as openly discussed as they are today. My mother was furious and horrified; she thought I was on the verge of joining 'some cult', as she put it. Now at the point of wondering if I needed help for mental health difficulties, I chose, like many others, not to discuss what was happening to me any more, with anyone. I just quietly apologized to my grandmother in my mind. I didn't know what else to do or how to take it further.

My experience is very similar to many of the stories I have heard from other people over the years. They, too, experience the initial fear and desire for their experiences to go away, especially as their family and friends also reject them in the early stages of psychic opening. Society on the whole is still afraid of the idea of psychic skills and ability, still sceptical of the idea that we have a deeper part of our nature and understanding, and often individuals with such abilities are shunned. This is perhaps due to many centuries of social conditioning about our understanding of God and the doctrines of the Church. My mother grew up in a quietly Catholic environment, educated by nuns and with a mother who practised her religion quietly. Both believed their natural sixth sense was something that must be denied. Perhaps because they believed it to be sinful, their religious conditioning made it difficult for them to move beyond what others thought, whether it was their parents, the priest, the Church or society in general.

Over the years I have watched many people go through tremendous guilt, at least initially, for discovering the intuitive side to their nature, or even wishing to do so. When working in southern Ireland I noticed the guilt in people was, at times, overpowering. In this amazing country, full of truly wonderful people, I came across two men I remember distinctly. Both were nervous about talking to me as a psychic and healer. One of them had suffered as a child at the hands of monks who had consistently beaten him with a leather strap at school because of his curiosity about the sixth sense and his wonder at how the universe works. The other was a Catholic priest, a delightful man but one who worried about being 'caught' talking to me. He had discovered a healing gift and wanted to know how he could develop it. Both worried about real or imagined repercussions of taking any advice I gave them. The first man went through a powerful release, and with tears pouring down his face he thanked me profusely for helping him understand there was nothing 'wrong' with him or his curiosity. The priest left with calm serenity after having satisfied his desire to start developing the wonderful healing energy he possessed. But both were deeply worried about the external consequences of telling people in their environments that they had been to see me.

Such fears are mainly due to our upbringing concerning what is 'evil' and to our struggle to move away from what other people think and towards thinking for ourselves. Such moves increase psychic and intuitive ability tenfold. The tenfold increase is due to the internal energetic channels clearing and a natural internal confidence building. The majority of people attending the psychic-development courses I have taught over the years have commented on how much their ability has increased, stabilized and become extremely useful, due to the results of actively engaging their psychic ability.

For myself and for others, I have seen a shift towards spiritual thinking as the most helpful. Spiritual thinking incorporates all beliefs regarding religion and ideas of God or the life source. Spiritual beliefs involve the idea that none of us is separate or judged as special or doomed because of what religious faith or ideas might tell us. Spiritual people generally have a lovely, peaceful demeanour; they are not critical or over-judgemental. This is not to say that spiritual people do not suffer from the same human shortfalls as others; rather, they are simply more aware of how negativity affects others. Stored judgements create bitterness, eventually harming the person storing the bitterness most of all. But it is not as simple as saying, 'Just let go of the past pattern that creates limitation,' because most people often need help releasing their limitations. Sometimes this might involve directed healing work from a therapist; for others, it is inspired through the 'opening' stages.

The energy of spiritual events, such as mind–body–spirit or complementary health festivals, is very pleasant to be in. The people who attend such festivals generally tend to be very calm individuals looking for like-minded people. They spend all day at such events taking in the atmosphere of gentleness.

Likewise, many spiritual texts claim that our psychic skills open, develop and sharpen as we lose our limiting beliefs and our tendency to hold on to past pain. This I believe to be true. In the classes that I teach, I have seen most people shift from the purely psychic dynamic into one that encompasses the spiritual as well as the psychic. Having done so, their innate gifts have increased tremendously and an amazing accuracy unfolds as the 'ego' self no longer dominates, but instead combines with the spiritual dimension of pure thought. The psychic or seer is then able to interpret information with confidence, rather than simply relying on direction from the ego self, which perhaps is more willing to please or pass on information judgementally.

A friend of mine is an example of this. He is a truly spiritual individual who has only recently acknowledged his psychic side. He struggles with the idea of a psychic reality due to the deeply logical nature of his work. He unwittingly passes on profound pieces of information as he combines the sixth sense with the pure thought that passes through his consciousness. He does not judge his thoughts but judiciously shares the information as it passes through. These thoughts prove to be very simple yet amazing, and they resonate with people deeply.

In contrast, a very good medium I know who has spent little time developing the spiritual side of her nature has now come across limitations in her ability to interpret the messages she receives. A mixture of challenges in her life that she finds difficult to cope with has meant her readings have become tainted with her own views and fears. She admits this as something she has noticed in recent times and is working hard on herself to resolve.

Many experience the fear of interpreting messages incorrectly or projecting their own issues on to others while passing on a message. This is a healthy fear in the early stages of development, and it shows a person who is aware of her possible limitations. Such fears are easily alleviated with a conscious effort to work on your own issues. We all carry heavy bags through life; it is part of the human experience. Once we begin to notice them and have a willingness to put them down, not only is life lighter but our ability to decipher the contents of other people's bags and help them to put them down becomes much easier.

When I did not know where to go with my experiences of spirit and my grandmother's increased presence, I went quiet for a few months, trying to busy myself and forget about the fact my mother thought I'd lost the plot. I continued to go about my life. At work one day during a dull data-entry task, I noticed I had been predicting the information coming next and entering it before I'd seen it. Believing it to be yet another coincidence, I made a few phone calls and found myself asking clients about products that hadn't been released yet. One asked me 'Heidi, are you psychic? That is not general information yet; how did you know that?' Of course I had no answer, just more confusion.

Confusion

Many of the strong psychic experiences people have stem from childhood or are a re-emergence of childhood abilities. For example, many children are incredibly sensitive to the words they hear adults say, and are often very intuitive as to the intended meaning. As a child, I assumed everyone knew that what people said was often not what they meant. I could never understand why someone would respond to what a person was *saying*, when what the person was *thinking* was the opposite. It would confuse me profoundly! I could also predict behaviours perfectly and adjust to them accordingly. Careful not to be noticed, I melted into the background into the inner world where I was at peace in the silence. The outer world saw me as a non-expressive and sensitive child who wouldn't join in.

I believe many people with a naturally deepened sensitivity to the intuitive side have had just such childhood experiences. Their imaginary friends, seen by many as part of a vivid imagination, are often, in fact, people in spirit who have formed friendships with the minds of children untainted by logic, mistrust or judgement. My sister, I remember, played with her imaginary friend 'Margery' for hours. I remember the beauty of her little voice talking with Margery, laughing and giggling. Unfortunately this is something she can no longer remember; the logic of schooling, work and life has taken over the mystical and magical part of her imagination. Likewise, many people are ashamed to let this part of them re-emerge; they lack trust in it and remain within the day-to-day logic of tasks and duties. Why? No wonder our society needs escapism.

After the strange 'coincidences' at work, I went home that evening looking for the phone book. I'd had enough of the confusion and lack of answers, so I began to look in the book for a Spiritualist church. I thought I would just sit at the back and observe what went on. Like most people, I was afraid of what I might find, thinking that the possible 'hocus-pocus' of it all would be frightening. What if I heard something I didn't want to? Even worse, what would my mother say?

Looking through the telephone book I had trouble finding a Spiritualist church, much less anyone who could possibly explain my experience. Eventually I found a Spiritualist church miles away from where I lived. About to dial the number, I heard a very loud voice say, 'No. Wait.' Startled, I did as I was told and put the phone book down.

CHAPTER 2
What Are Psychic Development and Intuition?

Much of the history of the word 'psychic' is wrapped up in connotation, mysticism and taboo. Some people associate the word psychic with fortune-telling or a traumatic injury, such as a bump on the head, that somehow makes you all-knowing and all-seeing. I have no recall of ever being whacked on the head, but I do have a highly intuitive skill and 'psychic' ability that I have developed over many years. For me it has been about developing a curiosity and willingness to investigate more of the potentially unknown, coupled with a strong desire to help people unveil a magical part of themselves which they will never regret finding.

To date, this philosophy has been highly beneficial, fulfilling my curiosity and helping people on their route forward in life, often exploring potential they'd never discovered before. It is not about telling people they are going to meet a tall, dark stranger or win the lottery. It is about exploring the energy of specific situations and the potential outcomes based on that energy moving forward. It's about how to deal happily with the inevitable, or looking at blocks within the psyche that prevent aspects of life as we progress, such as job opportunities or relationships.

These are things I have found over years of practice to be of great benefit to others.

A young woman came to see me who had been recommended by a family member. She was extremely upset and could hardly control her tears. Her partner of several years had dumped her some weeks previously. The reason he gave her was that, while she wanted children, he didn't want any more (he already had two from a previous relationship). This woman wanted help with how to deal with the mass of emotion passing through her. Calmly, I looked at the energy of the situation and felt very strongly that this man had deep feelings of love for this woman. I could also feel that the idea that he didn't want children wasn't true, although he did think strongly that it was. I could feel his real reasons had to do with bad experiences of marriage in the past and his fear over his two children from this previous marriage. He feared he did not spend enough time with them. His unconscious, it felt to me, was simply scared.

She said she wanted to leave and go back to her own country where she had family to support her, but she also felt she wanted to stay on in case he changed his mind. Strangely, I received specific instructions telling me how this woman should proceed. I told her the information, performed some healing work, and she left a lot calmer.

Approximately three months later she returned, this time even more hysterical than on the first occasion. 'He called like you said he would. I went back, though, too early. You told me to wait, I didn't listen. This time he says it's over for real.' Again, linking into the energy of his unconscious, I received the reply that this man was deeply in love with her. Listening intently to her energy, I was suddenly aware of a deep-seated fear within her psyche that was corresponding with her partner's fear. Interrupting her tears, I recalled to her the energy I was seeing.

It related to a time much earlier in her life. The energy was then released, much to her relief.

I then said, 'Listen, and listen carefully. I'm told if you follow these instructions all will be fine. These instructions will help him to release his fear and realize the deep love he has for you.' She went away and followed exactly the instructions I had received. Today, they are very happily married with a baby son.

I do not believe that any of what I do is a magical gift of any sort. I believe it is a result of actively developing my ability and skill in interpreting the unseen. I strongly believe we are surrounded by waves of energy that we are all capable of deciphering, if only we put our minds to it. I believe everything in the universe is connected and open for viewing; we just need to link into it. For correct interpretation, however, the link must be clear and free of interruption. The interruptions are our own fears, limitations and judgements that act as a filter for what would otherwise be pure energy ready for conversion into something tangible. The tangible is the truth, for energy cannot lie; it is only the interpretation that can be incorrect.

Psychic – Something Abnormal?

To be labelled 'psychic' in today's society often places a person as something out of the ordinary, even abnormal. Many people think it's mumbo-jumbo, a trick or the imagination. In my experience, none of the above is true. Yes, the interpretation some people give to the level of their particular skills can be a little dubious, but others are hugely modest and shy away from their potential.

Much of the fear around the word 'psychic' comes from history and a horror of the unknown. Like any profession, there are some unsavoury characters who are con artists, but the vast majority of psychics have a very genuine desire to help people.

Most psychics are like you or me, normal people who have come across a spontaneous opening process and have found their sixth sense. Mediums, on the other hand, specifically talk to those who have passed over. They offer possible evidence of life after death.

To be psychic simply means you have accessed an area of the self that most people never bother to pursue or actively identify. Yes, of course, some people are more naturally 'gifted' than others. To use a metaphor from running, any able-bodied person is capable of running at a moderate pace. Some are naturally fast runners, others have to work at it, and some just don't want to bother. But often, those who wish to can learn to run effectively and enjoy it to the extent they wouldn't want life to be any other way. They have their resistance moments, and having passed through those moments they can embrace and make the most of their skill.

A woman who spent years quietly attending one of the groups I teach didn't fully admit the level of her natural skill for some time. She attended classes for years, always enjoying them and gradually building her confidence. Culminating in attending the practitioner course, she finished as one of the best psychics/mediums I have ever come across. Calm, collected and very kind to her clients, today she very successfully helps the police find missing persons.

This woman started out like I did, with a curiosity and desire to understand something she couldn't quite grasp. The things she was seeing out of the corner of her eye, knowing of events before they happened and meeting spirits standing at the foot of her bed frightened and perplexed her. In the short term they were alarming experiences; in the long term, when she understood them, she actively controlled and developed them. As a result she now provides a very helpful, meaningful service for the police and the families of those missing.

At the other end of the scale, I meet a lot of people who have worked and worked for years, appearing never quite to master their intuitive skill and suddenly finding it bursting forth – once a level of self-development and acceptance prevails. These people attend the psychic-development workshops and classes for exactly the right reason: to enjoy themselves! Often this is all that is needed. Those I find who can take themselves lightly or allow themselves to lighten up develop their skill very quickly.

Society Teaches Head, Not Heart

As soon as we go to school, much of our sensitivity to our sixth sense is lost. This is because society teaches logic, practicality and 'common sense'. It is emphasized that we must accept only science rather than any form of intuitive instinct. Indeed, science is considered the only acceptable way of knowing, and the scientific method the only acceptable means of arriving at 'the truth'.

Many children come into this world with a powerful sixth sense and an ability to see and experience a connection with spirit. Many also have strong recollections of having 'been here before' in terms of past lives. There is strong evidence, throughout the world, of children recalling information they have not learned, thus suggesting the possibility of past lives.

When we go to school we are taught the essentials of reading, writing and mathematics, including the foundations of science, and we are told to trust only what can be proven through the scientific method. Imagination and fantasy are not encouraged, and sometimes they are even dismissed as escapist and inappropriate. We forget that most masters, from Mozart to Einstein, are famous for their daydreaming. This 'daydreaming' has been the source of fantastic inspiration that lies outside the realm of logic and reason. What a shame it is that imagination is not often encouraged in young children! How much better off would we all be if our imaginative and intuitive selves had been nurtured from a young age!

Interference from the 'Logical Mind'

It is likely that at some stage you will have interference from your 'logical' self. This is a normal part of the process until you become more familiar with the psychic part of yourself.

Interference from your logical mind means the discounting of truly psychic experiences, explained away as products of your vivid imagination. You may censor or disqualify psychic experiences by dismissing them as mere coincidence, chance or luck. You may not even think your psychic experiences are glamorous enough to mention. In reality a psychic event doesn't have to be big to be real. Actually the 'big deals' are rare; psychic awareness has more to do with an unending series of 'small deals' that make life easier and far more magical. When you wake up to your soul, you realize how much you are being guided and protected by higher planes of existence at all times. Such guidance is in direct contact with your soul energy. At times it will conflict with your reason, so when this happens don't be surprised that the small, still voice will speak up loudly. It will throw pebbles at you, and if you ignore the pebbles it throws bricks, and if you ignore the bricks, it will throw a huge boulder. Wouldn't you rather heed the pebbles?

What I call the logical mind has its place within our psyche. It is there to help distil truth from imagination or perceived thought based on the past. But too much logic gets in the way of strong intuitive skills and psychic development. Everyone at the beginning of actively developing his or her psychic skills is very conscious of the logical mind constantly questioning whether the experience is real or imagined. Too much focus on the logical slows one's process of learning how to trust intuitive skills and allowing them to develop.

I remember the first time I practised psychometry on a friend of mine. This involves holding jewellery to pick up a person's energy from the metal. My friend, whom I hadn't seen for a while, was sitting in a pub with me. She asked me to see if I could get anything from her ring. I sat with it for a short while, and suddenly I began to see bright green lizards all stuck to a concrete wall in a long corridor. Ignoring it, my logic believing it must be part of my vivid imagination, I continued to try to gain some information from the ring.

After ten minutes or so I told my friend about the luminous green lizards stuck to the concrete wall. Thinking it was completely ridiculous, I was embarrassed that I was even telling her. Gasping in amazement with her mouth wide open, she proceeded to tell me about her trip away in Turkey teaching English as a foreign language. Her room, she told me, was along a corridor of concrete walls. Along this corridor every evening were lots of bright green lizards stuck to the walls for the night.

Generally as humans we forget we are a spirit with a body rather than a body with a spirit. When we allow ourselves to function from the spirit, great things happen. An aspect of the self begins to unwind and show itself as something all-knowing, even though we have the filter of the logical mind.

Strong Blocks to Psychic Skills and How to Correct Them

One of the strongest blocks to a person's intuition and psychic ability is a hugely disorganized life. Intuition and psychic awareness are the ability to receive and perceive subtle direction from your higher self. If you live a life constantly in a state of disarray with unfinished business and projects half-started, it is unlikely you will receive guidance easily, even in the most obvious of circumstances. However, being organized does not mean you are automatically and consistently psychic. Psychic ability is a relay between your conscious mind and your higher self. For that relay to occur consistently, you must first be able to reflect upon your present circumstances. If you are buried under too many responsibilities and demands, there is no time for reflection.

Organizing your life goes back to your intentions. Organization will follow your true intentions in life. Your true intentions are the things you really care about. Once organized, take 15 minutes a day to reflect upon them and your psychic abilities will, without doubt, improve significantly.

A Quiet Mind – Key to Developing Intuition

Being at a noisy party with lots of chatter all around you makes it very difficult, if not impossible, to hear someone trying to have a conversation with you. At a library, where it is generally very quiet, when a person speaks at the other end of the room every word is crystal-clear. If someone shouts in such an environment his voice booms for all to hear.

When communicating with the intuitive part of the self, the higher self, to spirit guides or to those who have passed from this life to the next, it is very challenging to hear them if you have a party going on in your head. Part of developing strong psychic or intuitive skills is the discipline of quieting the mind. Similar to most things in life, once you get used to actively quieting the mind it soon becomes automatic. Life becomes very easy; any subtle communications can be heard clearly. Any messages from spirits can be passed on accurately, as the energy can be interpreted with little interference.

How to Quiet the Mind

Meditation is body-building for the mind. It is known extensively for helping to create inner peace, harmony and relief from the stress of everyday life. Many people are reluctant to meditate because they believe they cannot do it, haven't time for it, or that it's boring.

Once you are in the swing of meditation it is an incredibly life-enhancing experience. Guided meditations are an easy way to develop the skill and for you to have some direction during your meditation practice.

For the beginner it is advisable to spend no more than about five minutes following a guided meditation. This is because your conscious attention span is very limited when your mind is busy. If a meditation is only five minutes long, most people can stick with it and follow the process without their mind wandering or without falling asleep. If you already have the psychic-development home course I provide, you will find the meditations very helpful. They are purposely short, and the sound behind each one helps to quiet the mind with little effort since the accompanying music is set for the brainwaves to respond and quieten to a relaxed state. (There's more about meditation in Chapter 8.)

Persistence pays off. After only a few weeks of relaxation meditation even the busiest of minds will slow down and take you ever closer to the 'library'.

Thoughts about how you feel or how someone has upset you during your day can go round and round in your head. To quiet this, a helpful process that also connects you to your truest and deepest feelings is to write out all that you feel. Start a sheet of paper or a computer document with a sentence. Something to help get you started, perhaps, would be, 'I feel angry today because ...' Let the pen flow or let your typing fingers dance. Keep going until there is nothing left, no more feelings to state, or when you begin to wander on to something else. The angry feelings will soften and disappear. Once your writing for the day is complete, there is no need to read it. Tear it up, throw it away or delete it from your computer.

CHAPTER 3
What It's Like to Be Psychic

Information for the People

When I actively began to receive psychic information about people and situations, my mother became frightened. I remember one occasion distinctly when she 'told' me to give up psychic-development classes. I was trying to share with her some of the experiences I had started to have. We both had horses, and I was grooming my horse when I thought discussing psychic phenomena might be appropriate. I knew she received psychic information on occasion, as she sometimes spoke about 'one of her feelings', so I assumed it would be OK to bring the subject up. I couldn't have been more wrong! She couldn't cope with the types of things I was describing; they were too 'real'. When things remained as 'one of her feelings', it felt safe to her.

Over the years I have come to discover there are certain patterns that occur when someone is beginning to open up to the psychic self. The first and most basic is receiving information about or for another person. I remember as a child getting into trouble for speaking thoughts people had not apparently expressed. I would get confused with what was thought and what was said. I could hear the thoughts and feelings of a person as though they were my own thoughts. I assumed everyone knew what went on in another person's head, even if that person didn't say it. Sometimes I would 'hear' these thoughts as though the other person had really spoken them out loud, hence my confusion. My mother would scold me for expressing what she thought was an unkind interpretation of what a person had said. She would tell me the other person hadn't said what I had heard. I would argue, of course, and within a few days or weeks my argument would prove true.

I know there are many people walking around on this planet who do the same thing I've always done and assume, like me, that everyone can listen to, or spontaneously hear, the thoughts of another person. It is not until they hit their adult years that they realize not everyone is a 'mind-reader'. This 'mind-reading' progresses to receiving information for friends and family, often accompanied by a desperate urge to pass it on. Many avoid this urge for fear of being labelled 'crazy' or 'unstable', only to find out later that it would have been really quite useful if they had passed the message on. At school I would comment on my friends' choices of boyfriends. It would spontaneously come out of my mouth. For teenagers it is often difficult to keep quiet about information you have received – call it naiveté – but you soon learn to keep quiet after feeling the wrath of your closest mates for whom you've hit a little too close to home. I would find myself saying what the strengths and weaknesses of the relationship would be and how long it would last based on the characteristics of both individuals. I was usually right. After a few years, even through rose-tinted glasses and gritted teeth, friends would come to me with their new boyfriends. I then had to give them my 'comment', as they had ceased to bother forcing something that wasn't going to work, or wanted to know when they could relax into something that would.

Dreams

Precognitive dreams are a very clear sign of spontaneous psychic development. This is seeing things in dreams before they happen. For many this can be a scary idea, mostly because we are afraid of seeing something unpleasant or unfortunate. With spiritual development and a better understanding of what is happening to you, it becomes less frightening and less of a burden. It is important to remember that sometimes these precognition dreams are best interpreted *symbolically* rather than literally. Therefore, a mind full of fear will interpret the information fearfully, but a mind without fear can often see what the symbolism really represents.

I remember distinctly the first two times I received information in dreams. In the first one I saw a plane crash and bodies floating in the sea, and I had the sense this plane had been blasted out of the sky. I mentioned it to my mother. I could even see the faces of the people floating! To my absolute horror, three days later I heard on the news about a plane that had been blasted out of the sky by some sort of land-based missile in the US. The plane had landed in the sea and all the passengers had died either on impact or by drowning. The description, including the name of the airline, matched what I had seen. My mother found what I had said disconcerting, especially since there was no question that I had 'pre-seen' the event. I had mentioned all the facts days before the crash appeared on the news.

Due to the fact I had become more aware of energies without realizing it, I was spontaneously linking to an 'energy-taking form'. This is common for someone just opening up to the psychic self. As you begin to develop your psychic skills and become able to link into the energies you choose to link into, rather than spontaneously linking into the strongest energy at a given time, such occurrences happen much less often.

Dreams are also a fantastic way for spirits to make initial contact. For someone new to psychic development or frightened of his skill, spirits will use dreams as a meeting ground. This is because the astral planes are more accessible when we are relaxed. During a sleep state it is easy for you to meet loved ones (who have passed) or to have a message passed on to you via the astral plane. I have heard many stories of people meeting their loved ones for a conversation while dreaming. For some, a telephone is used in the dream; for others it is a deep and vivid conversation in a face-to-face meeting. The loved one usually mentions being 'fine' and may pass on a word of advice either for the person dreaming or for some other person known to them.

Dreams also increase in frequency and intensity the more you concentrate on developing psychic skills. This is due to your psyche using your dreams as an opportunity to have a clearing-out. Old 'files' in the mind that are no longer required are rifled through and emptied in the sleep state. Some people may go through a period of intense, sometimes unpleasant, dreams. These are to be celebrated rather than dreaded, for your psyche is very effectively sorting what it wants to use and keep while throwing out the rest. Your psyche is developing the ability to receive subtle energies. The blocking energies are disposed of, and some of these vivid experiences may stay with you for days, weeks, even a lifetime.

There is a period of getting used to being on the astral planes during the sleep state. Indications of this happening are an increase in dreams, also the meeting of loved ones in dreams, but more importantly the feeling of a 'crash landing' back into your body when you awake. This is when you are aware of being awake or feel as though you have your eyes open when they are still closed. This can feel as though there is a presence in the room and you can't breathe. The presence can feel menacing, and you may feel very scared. There is, in fact, no presence in the room; what has happened is that you have woken up before the astral body has realigned correctly. A deep breath and a relaxing thought of 'I'm OK' will sort it out immediately.

Fascination

Having a fascination for the psychic sciences is another strong indication of the sixth sense opening up. This can range from being interested in mediums to having quite a few readings. Such a fascination is associated with the psyche wanting more explanation for this side of life in order to minimize fears trapped in the personality. It is also a desire of the logical self to seek strong 'proof' of a life beyond the five senses. This fascination is often evident in childhood, either through an ability to see things others can't or through repressing it completely. An emotionally mature psyche cautiously opens up again by testing the waters and strengthening belief through developing a fascination with psychic skills. For others, it is a fascination with the world of apparent fantasy through fairies, pixies and other nature spirits. As a child I was completely drawn to anything of a fairy nature. This fascination has never left me, and even into my adult years I still love to collect fairy figures.

Attraction to Light Colours

When people allow the psyche to open up to the sixth sense, they often go through what I call 'the pink and purple phase'. During this phase people find themselves attracted to pale colours, particularly pink, purple and white. You may find yourself buying a new wardrobe of everything either purple or pink or having a desire to paint the walls in your home lilac.

My husband remembers my 'pink' phase distinctly. On our first meeting I was wearing huge, bright pink sparkling boots. I loved those boots at the time; only years later did I realize quite how 'pink' they were!

The attraction to such light colours is indicative of the upper chakras extending themselves and opening up. The attraction to pink is the heart centre opening and balancing, which is an important and necessary part of extending the ability of the third eye. While the heart centre is balancing itself it is possible for you to feel a strong tightness in the chest, followed by a release of emotion that seems to come from nowhere. This lasts for a short period of time and is not associated with depression.

Wanting more lilac is about the third eye expanding. As the sixth sense opens up, the third eye needs 'feeding' with more energetic frequencies of the colour lilac. This can be followed by a pulling and stretching sensation across the forehead.

The need for more white comes from the crown chakra expanding its connection to the life source. For most, this is God, a universal energy or a deity. Physically, the crown's opening can feel as though you have tiny fingers gently lifting your hair, or a tingling sensation on the top of your head. It is important to remember that not everyone experiences this part of the opening process, but many do.

The Different Experiences of Meeting Spirit

'Spirit' is the general term used for those who have passed from this life into what we commonly refer to as death. Much of our understanding of death is superstition and fear-based, and it arises from the practical observation that after death a person 'isn't here any more'. But that is a far different thing than saying that after death the *spirit* no longer exists. In psychic awakening we are made aware that a person lives on in spirit form after the body that contained the spirit expires.

There are various ways for spirits to make themselves known to people. If you imagine that the only way for spirit to make itself known is in physical form, then you are quite mistaken.

Apparitions appear as figures that are more see-through than the average human being. This is because they show themselves in what is called *the etheric body*. When a person dies he is cut free from this shell, otherwise known as the physical body, and released into the etheric body. The etheric body is an exact blueprint of the physical form, only lighter. When spirits show themselves in the etheric body they can adjust to fit your perception of them. If you remember them at a certain time, younger, brighter or happier, they are likely to show themselves in that form.

Apparitions are comparatively rare, since it takes a lot of effort for spirits to show themselves in a physical form. I will provide a clear explanation of an earth bound spirit later. However, when spirits do show themselves it is often for a particular purpose, perhaps to highlight something or to make it clear that they do still exist. Many show themselves shortly after death for a short time; this is to say goodbye. If a spirit does show itself in a physical form, it is often in the early hours of the morning or late at night. This is because most people are generally relaxed at this time of day, so are more likely to be in a receptive state to see them.

When I was first developing my psychic skills I often used to see people standing at the end of my bed. Most of the time they would just stand there; other times they would say something, usually my name, so clearly that I couldn't question it. The spirits were rarely someone I knew personally, for at the time I was not aware of many people who had passed over. They would stand there and smile. After a while I became a little spooked and would throw the duvet over my head and tell them to go away. They would come until I firmly believed spirits do exist. After that, they left me alone.

Feeling Spirit

When I firstly consciously felt spirit it was as though someone was permanently looking over my shoulder, as if peeking while I was reading an imaginary newspaper. Initially I assumed I was paranoid, until aspects of what I was experiencing were explained to me. The rest of my knowledge regarding spirits comes from years of experience.

It was explained to me that spirits occupy the same space as we do. They do not exist in the sky, or somewhere else, but on a finer vibration not immediately accessible to the naked eye. The space is approximately three feet above our space, which is why spirits that present in the form of ghosts seem to be hovering. When there are a lot of spirits present, or when a form is taking shape, there will often be a strong temperature change. This is because in order for spirits to maintain a strong physical presence, they have to draw upon the earth's energies. The more they are occupying the immediate space, the cooler the temperature. With the presence of angels, as opposed to humans, this coolness is often accompanied by a strong smell of flowers, usually lilies. It is important to remember that the coolness is not indicative of anything threatening, which is what many people assume. It simply means that spirits are present.

Feeling the presence of spirits can feel as though someone has walked straight through you. To a certain extent, you may find they have. Spirits will quite often do so while trying to communicate a message. There may be an indication of some of the emotions they experienced as a living person, or spirits may give you an indication of what they died of, not through speech but through feeling.

Here's an illustration. A man came to see me some years ago; he wanted to see if his father would communicate with me. His father did come, and though he was not a talkative chap he did attempt to make it clear to his son that it was indeed he by showing me what he had died of. Initially I was confused, as my body felt pelted by tiny prickles all over it. I tried desperately to work out what it was. Again I was bombarded with prickles. I knew he was trying to communicate what he had died from, but, like a game of charades, I was avidly trying to work out what he meant. I told his son what I was feeling. The son said it was certainly him, and that he had died during the troubles in Northern Ireland. He had been shot repeatedly and had died from his wounds. Ah, I thought, bullets. That's what the prickles were.

Persistent Message

Sometimes spirits will try to gain your attention by repeating a message. For me it is often the repetition of a sentence, image, individual words or a name. If I am communicating with spirits for someone, dismissing something as irrelevant will result in my mind seeing a set of pictures or a name. If the message is for me, they will be repeated over and over again. Once I take heed, they leave me alone. This happens for me on almost a daily basis. If the message is for someone else, perhaps a friend, they will not leave me until I have called that person.

A few years ago I had such a communication, practically in the middle of the night. In the end I called the friend of mine for whom the message was intended. He was on the other side of the world, so my night-time call didn't disturb him. I told him to sell 80 per cent of his shares. I had been told that unless he did so immediately he would lose every penny of the money he had tied up in the shares. He told me not to be so ridiculous; shares were going up, and he was *making* money, certainly not *losing* it! I told him in a very stern voice, 'Just do it. Do as you're told.' I don't know who was helping him out that day, but sure enough he did what he was told immediately. Two days after my phone call the US stock market crashed when the 'dot com' companies folded (May 2000). The 20 per cent he kept made millions, as it was one of the few stocks that went up when everything was going down. If he hadn't sold the other shares, he would have lost everything.

I have had plenty of forewarning from spirits through words being repeated over and over in my head until I took notice. One such occasion was during the time I was pregnant. At five months a single word kept repeating itself to me, a word having to do with my pregnancy. I had no idea what the word meant but, having it repeated constantly in my head, I decided to look it up. It was 'pre-eclampsia'. I learned about it, what it was, what the signs were, and the word in my head stopped. Knowing that for some reason I had needed to know what it was, I then forgot about it. Towards the end of my pregnancy I began to look really quite ill. I was incredibly swollen, so swollen that people didn't recognize me. My midwife sent me to hospital for a check-up scan as she couldn't feel where the baby was. Then the word started in my head again, so I calmly went to hospital knowing what was going on. I was fully informed because of my research three months earlier and was immediately admitted with the life-threatening pre-eclampsia. If I had not had the forewarning I would have been very frightened, but because I knew what it was I was able to focus on allowing my body to relax and accept treatment. Within three days the doctors let me go home. The consultant said he had no idea what had happened! All the signs were indicating significant pre-eclampsia, yet I had recovered very quickly. He told me I had been admitted with significant health problems, which they'd thought were going to require drastic measures. But my blood pressure was able to return to normal and I went home to finish my pregnancy.

For many people spirits communicate like this every day. They drop helpful hints and valuable information into our consciousness. Most of us, though, are not listening. We wander around in an unconscious daze, barely listening to ourselves let alone guidance from an external source.

There are several ways to improve your ability to 'listen and feel' when spirits are offering help.

Speaking to Spirit

For most people it takes a while to realize that much of the information we receive from spirit helpers is not our imagination. I know that even today my psyche faces a battle between what is real and what is imagined. The challenge that takes place in the mind is very much a healthy challenge; it gives us the ability of discernment, a natural requirement in this day and age.

Speaking to spirits is different from speaking to your friend or next-door neighbour, even if you see a spirit in a physical form. Rarely do spirits speak with their mouths; they speak with their minds. Spoken communication with the spirit world is through telepathy, a communication from mind to mind. This communication can be very clear and obvious, or it can feel very distant, like a pause. The pause feels like a long-distance phone call before satellite; there is a slight delay in the relay of messages. That relay between this world and the spirit world gets easier to predict and to decipher as you become more experienced at receiving messages. God gave you two ears and one mouth. Use them in that order.

There are many ways to improve your ability to feel and hear spirits better. The methods that help you to decipher real from imagined communication helps you to recognize your psyche's way of receiving information from an outside influence.

Working consistently on quieting your mind is essential for all forms of psychic development. When communicating with a spirit it is vital to be able to tune in to a voice or impression from outside your own mind. Spirit communication is not always loud and clear. Some parts can seem distant, or you may have to strain to hear. For other people, or at other times, the communication can be a booming in your ears or head.

Hearing spirits can also be a subtle communication, a kind of unspoken knowing. This sense of knowing can become stronger as you become more used to communication from the other side. Knowing your own mind is a very clear pointer to communication with spirits. Many people who are spontaneously developing their psychic abilities or who have a keen interest in doing so find that they have a better understanding of themselves. If you are a person who has no idea what you want from life or are afraid to go after what is important to you, then contact from spirits is going to scare you. You may wish it would all go away, only to find yourself actively searching for deeper spiritual meaning in some other way, for example by reading this book. Be advised: the more you avoid it, the stronger it will get. The urge to have a better understanding of what is important in your life will eventually back you into a corner until you embrace it. This is not to annoy you; it is a necessary area for growth, especially if part of your life plan is to take direction from more evolved souls in order to enhance your own.

If developing your communication skills with the spirit plane of existence is part of your conscious plan, then learning how to make sense of yourself becomes easier. This is because you will leave fear at the door as you pursue your interest in finding what you want. Part of the process may involve sorting out the things in life that you *don't* want and that you wish to change.

Spirits need the clearest passage possible for their messages. Thus someone who knows himself well becomes very appealing to spirits because they can be more certain of a clearly delivered message. That is why a quiet mind is so important!

Quieting the mind is possible through meditation and spending quiet 'alone' time with yourself. This alone time only needs to be a short period; even five minutes a day makes a difference. Guided meditation is best for the beginner. A quiet mind does not guarantee that spirits will communicate with you, but it makes a tremendous difference to the possibility that they will – and will also help you in other areas of your life.

From the Higher Self

At the early stages of the opening process I have noticed numerous people finding themselves under the strong direction of the higher self. The higher self is the higher mind; it is a vital part that most people never really consciously use. It ignites unconsciously when the body is in extreme circumstances or danger. It is the part responsible for those cases you hear of in which people have acquired amazing strength, as when you hear of an old woman suddenly being able to lift a car off an injured child.

The higher self is the part of you that you know exists. It is the part that knows the truth of any situation, deep down.

During the 'opening' process people tend to find they are directed towards operating from this higher part of themselves, this 'higher consciousness'. Living their 'real truth' is the only option.

Chaos can occur during the transition phase as all that operates from an untruth starts to be eradicated. This can mean that everything starts to change in your life. Relationships built on thin ice can collapse, sometimes rather dramatically, and things you've tried to compartmentalize or fit into defined boxes no longer conform. People won't behave in the way you want them to; the ability of others to manipulate you suddenly doesn't work any more. Everyone does or has tried to manipulate a situation or person at some point in life, and you haven't escaped it! Friendships change; you no longer want acquaintances because you now want only friends in your life, relationships built on truth. Your job may change even if you didn't mean for it to change! You may start to panic as it can start to feel that your life is out of control. Perfect! It is only then that you can really take charge and operate from what you actually want in life rather than simply react to what life brings to you.

I remember when my higher self really activated as the part of me that operates my life. It happened when I stopped resisting it. One day I gave up resisting the fact that I was going into the unconventional world of Spiritualism and personal growth. Being a practical person, this was very difficult for me. The day I gave up the resistance was when I said, 'OK, give it to me. Whatever I must change in order to move forward I will. I give in, and I will not resist. I trust it is for my higher good, no matter what the consequences. Resisting is too much work.'

Within two months I had lost my home, contact with my family, my job, my precious horse, my car and my boyfriend. This all sounds rather extreme, right? Yes it does, and perhaps by now you are feeling some worry about your own life changing to such an extent. I admit that at the time it was a horrendous experience, but I trusted I would find my way clear. It was not a naïve sort of trust based on hope but a trust based on 'knowing' that I would find my absolute truth as a result of what was happening.

Now I know it was the most wonderful opportunity I have ever had. The period of time without contact with my family was necessary for them to accept my life and work choices. The change of job was so that I could do what I do now and have done ever since. Losing my horse was the end of a wonderful partnership, but losing the car meant I had more flexibility to repay my student and graduate debts, which I did in under a year. My boyfriend needed the time to work out what he wanted in his life. This was something I was upset about at the time, but even though it hurt I managed to let it go. That boyfriend returned to me as a man, and I am delighted to say he is now my wonderful husband. So, although the changes brought about by the higher self can be drastic and frightening, if you are prepared to trust the outcome and accept these as opportunities rather than crises, then you have a perfect springboard to a very rewarding existence.

CHAPTER 4
The Process of Psychic Development and Finding a Group

Openness

I remember distinctly the first psychic-development class I attended. The room was filled with very friendly people from all walks of life. As the class began people were describing experiences I could immediately recognize and understand. Here was a whole room full of people openly talking about all those things that my mother had previously criticized me for discussing even with just her! I felt at home.

The number-one part of the process of psychic development, the most fundamental and essential starting point, are an openness and willingness to learn. Like anything in life, those who believe they know it all, those who answer questions with a volley of 'yes, buts', actually develop slowest. I believe it is because the 'lower self', or personality, is dictating their progress rather than allowing themselves to trust the higher mind. Those who are open and willing, even if they have no previous experience of psychic development, progress very quickly and are a delight to work with.

When I attended that first psychic-development class I knew nothing about the subject. All I knew was that I had had experiences that I wanted explained. I went in with an open mind, but to be truthful I was expecting an event full of slightly 'far out' people. What I saw was a group of wonderful, normal people in a class led by an unbelievably normal woman. This environment made it very safe for me to allow my curiosity to run wild.

Curiosity

The most psychic people I know are extremely curious. They are curious about people, situations and how a person's life turns out. They also have a brilliant memory for people and their lives. The name of a person is extremely important. People love for you to remember their name, and I believe it is a very polite and easy thing to do. I have noticed that those who remember names and have a deep curiosity turn out to be very good psychics and mediums. The reason why this is so is unclear, but I believe it's because those developing their sixth sense have a naturally empathetic inclination and a strong interest in people's lives. This makes them a sponge for information, both spoken and unspoken. I may go for years without speaking to or seeing a person who has asked for my help or for a reading, but in the majority of cases when they re-contact me every detail of that person's life or the reading I gave will pop into my head. It will run like a movie through my head. The names, the images and the places will often immediately re-ignite in my third eye. Then curiosity drives me forward into the next part of their lives with which they require guidance.

Developing curiosity is simple. For you it may be natural and something that requires little effort. For others it may well be something that needs a little stimulation. When I was first developing my psychic skills I would gaze at people as I travelled on the train to university. I would wonder what their lives were like, imagining their interests, their goals in life and what they wished for. I never knew if I was right because, obviously, I never asked them, but I would have a stream of images passing through my head, along with a bundle of feelings passing through my solar plexus. I would use these as 'practice', as a way of recognizing how to match images with emotions. What I practised on the train I'd then take into my learning environment, and when I would link into things I was asked to link into I'd find the information would start up in exactly the same way as when I practised on the train. The way I learned to develop my curiosity won't work for everyone, for nothing scared me. If you are very sensitive, however, practising on people in your environment may not be for you. Also, when you do link into strangers, consider their privacy. I only chose to link into parts of their psyche that they were willing to share.

A Deepened Interest in the Unseen

A strong interest in the unseen is an obvious sign of someone with a psychic ability beyond the everyday levels of instinct most people have. The reason for this interest in the unseen arises because part of our psyche wishes to open up and become more aware of the unseen energies that exist in our environment. I believe it is also linked to a natural part of the evolutionary process. We have learned how to produce goods and provide a roof over our heads. The next part of human development is to expand the capability of our minds. Such things as technology and the Internet are intangible; you can't feel them but you can see the end result. For continued development into something as miraculous as technological breakthroughs, the mind needs to expand. A deepened interest in the unseen allows for people to open up into an arena not accessed before and to reach a level of creativity beyond our present perception.

An Increase in Coincidence

There is a distinct increase in positive coincidence and being in the right place at the right time. For most people this increases steadily from the beginning of their psychic-development process through to the day they leave the planet. An increase in our ability to accept both inner and outer guidance accounts for this change. As we become more trusting of the process, our ability to manifest what we want in life becomes a normal event. This can mean anything from manifesting a box of tissues when you need them to receiving a new car without much effort.

When I was new to psychic development I remember standing outside a hotel in London waiting for a taxi. Manifesting was also something I was not used to. Usually, like everyone else, most of what I wanted either eluded me or I had to wait ages for it. Outside the hotel on a freezing winter evening, taxis were in short supply. I looked across at a brand new chauffeur-driven Bentley as the passengers left their car, and wondered what it would be like to get home in a taxi that was a Bentley. At that instant, the driver got out of the car and popped his head over the roof. He was dressed from head to foot in a chauffeur's uniform, including the hat. He called over to me, 'Would you like a lift home?' Looking around, checking that he was talking to me, I said, 'Yes, please.' The woman standing next to me happened to live the next street away from me, so we both hopped into the Bentley. I can still remember, even now, thinking, 'Why on earth is this man being so kind, driving us 20 miles out of his way?' Some call it luck. I call it manifesting.

Indeed, manifesting is extraordinary when it works in its most elaborate form. I did not ask anyone for anything; I simply wondered, while bored, freezing and waiting for a taxi, what it would be like to go home in a Bentley. As the stagnant energy disperses, manifesting can be only a thought away.

Everything Goes Quiet, Then Starts Up Again

Many people have commented over the years that they can experience a huge amount of psychic activity followed by a 'slump' or a desire to steer clear of it because it's all a bit much. My advice is, if you have been having a lot of unsettling psychic experiences, the best thing you can do to make it settle down is to take an interest in it. The more you understand something, the less frightened you become. For those who naturally and spontaneously 'open up', it is important you grasp the process of it all. This is so you can choose and discern the types of energy you wish to channel. Many people in the early days of their psychic development make the mistake of thinking that if spirits talk to them, or if they receive messages for other people, then they must pass them on or accept visits from ghostly strangers in the middle of the night simply because they have this 'gift'. It is not true. As in life, those who have passed over have no right over you. You have the same freedom of choice as you have in every other aspect of your life. You can choose whom you wish to communicate with, just as in life, and if you do not want to talk to frightening or unsavoury characters or accept them in your space you don't have to. You are under no obligation to entertain these 'bad' spirits simply because they reveal themselves to you.

For those who do try to avoid their psychic side, whether through choice, fear or beliefs within their families, no matter how much they try to bury this dimension of their personality it will come up again. There is no time limit attached to this. Many people I have spoken to or taught in classes have had an interest in psychic development for as long as they can remember, having found that even if it goes quiet for a while it all starts up again when they least expect it. This is because the soul's urge is still present, and the quiet period is simply due to its taking a holiday.

Impulse for Continuous Self-improvement

During the drive towards exploring your sixth sense, you will find yourself with a bug for self-improvement. This will take different forms based on the type of person you are. Generally the drive will include the following:

- a desire to reduce the amount of meat you eat
- low/lower tolerance of foods you eat too much of
- a repulsion for junk food that you didn't have previously
- lower alcohol tolerance
- continued fascination for any form of self-development
- stronger desire to explore new territory
- inability to keep still; a desire to be busy
- increase in creativity
- low tolerance for things that do not sit well
- reduction in procrastination.

These are only some of the main forms people generally experience; there are many others. The change in food fancies and tolerance tends to be a result of an increase in energy vibration, which perhaps you wish to maintain. Therefore, the body starts to generate a move towards increasing the generally higher frequency and vibration, which often requires a 'cleaner' system.

Think of this as a metaphor: if you never clean your car, it still works; but over time the bodywork becomes dull, lifeless and ultimately rusted. If you had looked after the car, no matter what its age, it would still gleam. Energy vibrations work in a similar way: the more you 'clean' them, the brighter the sparks. When the whole system of a person has experienced 'cleaning' through aspects of psychic and spiritual development, there is a natural, often unconscious, desire to maintain this.

Choosing a Psychic-development Group

There are many psychic-development groups around. Some of these are easy to locate; others are hidden away. When choosing a group it is important to go to one you feel comfortable in. The best groups are ego-free and have the philosophy that everyone is equal. The group I started with when I was new and scared made me feel immediately welcome. It was full of lovely, very friendly people. Choose a group who will give you this feeling, and be mindful and respectful of them also.

The best way to find a group is through personal recommendation. If you have friends who rave about the group they are with, go to that one. If you do not have that luxury, then there are other ways to find a group. For example, Spiritualist churches are a source of information. However, they focus mainly on mediumship rather than other forms of psychic phenomena. You will find with many of them that their development groups are closed circles, but others do have open circles, so it is worth asking. If you want your learning to be easy on the wallet, then finding a Spiritualist church is your answer, as many of their meetings charge only a minimal fee. However, some Spiritualist churches have what could be described as 'old thinking' that doesn't particularly suit those interested in incorporating a deep self- and spiritual development. This is not true of all Spiritualist churches but is something to be aware of.

Other psychic-development groups are set up by practising psychics and mediums. These are worth investigating and visiting to see if you are suitable for the group. A good fit should enable you to feel comfortable from the outset, even if a little scared. Finding these in your area can be a challenge, but mind–body–spirit magazines are a good source.

A psychic-development group should be something you enjoy. If you feel pressurized or bored, then you need to find something that fits you better. If a group is going at a pace slower than you prefer, then change, as this will affect your interest and interaction in the group.

The classes and workshops that I teach start people off on the same level. They are known for both speed and depth, which most people have not come across before. I start always on the assumption that everyone is psychic but to differing levels, and I proceed to show through various meditations and exercises how psychic skills are so variable. The classes are light-hearted and full of laughter, as I'm not one for being ultra-serious. This helps people to immediately feel comfortable, and I love to watch people growing in confidence as the class goes on. This seems to be a very popular format. I use it because of the way I remember feeling when I first joined a psychic-development class, so I believe it is very important for people to gain confidence and belief in themselves if nothing else. However, this format is not for everyone, and you may prefer a more serious approach, which is why it is important for you to stick with a group you feel comfortable with.

The Internet is another option for finding resources and contacts. My websites, PsychicCourses.com and HeidiSawyer.com, offer free forums for asking questions to do with psychic development. Many people the world over who have either attended my courses or have the home version use the forums frequently. The forums are very helpful to those who wish to contact like-minded individuals for advice and support. You can also sign up for the free newsletter, which sends you useful tips for psychic development to help you along the way.

CHAPTER 5
When Choosing A Psychic – Consider ...

Good Psychics

A definition of a good psychic is often a personal choice. There are some definite traits to look for and some distinct ones to avoid.

Good psychics are realistic and in touch with themselves and reality. It is important to remember there is a difference between a psychic and a medium. Recall that a medium speaks to those who have passed over and attempts to give evidence of life after death. A psychic reads energy from its present position into its future expression. Some people are more than capable of doing both, but tend to have a preferred area. A brilliant psychic can see energy in its current position, and how they can clear it where it is not working for an individual.

A friend of mine is a brilliant psychic. Mediumship is not her preferred area but she is great at that also. We both have a very similar style that works for a lot of people who are interested in self-development, especially spiritual development. I remember watching a specific reading she did for a woman struggling with her weight. In less than five minutes this woman understood something she had never grasped before. My friend was able to give her the psychological specifics of why she was overweight and at what point in her life it had all started. It related back to an argument she had witnessed as a child. The argument was relayed by my friend to this woman, and in remembering its source she burst into tears. Three months later I learned that the woman concerned had lost nearly three stone without dieting. Her eating and exercise habits changed almost overnight with a simple adjustment in her energy field. This is not to say that powerful energy techniques work for everyone, but I have seen the use of energy by psychics within the scope of my friend's work, my own work and the work of other psychics, allowing for the creation of tremendous adjustments in a person.

Spotting Experienced and Ethical Psychics

Experienced and highly ethical psychics accept that they are not perfect and would not expect you to accept every word they utter. Everyone has free will; psychics can give guidance, often very specific guidance, on areas of a person's life that they are not yet completely familiar with. This is not to say everything has to turn out in the exact form a psychic has stated. Often a great psychic is reading energy already in motion. This is an energy that has already taken form; some aspects will be part of the individual's plan, others will be adjustable by free will. Experienced psychics are able to tell the difference between planned energy in motion and aspects a person can choose to change, which are often dependent on an inner adjustment of beliefs or attitudes.

A woman I had known for a while came to see me to ask about how likely it was going to be for her to meet a partner. She had been to see me several times previously asking similar questions. Each time, the guidance I had received for her was to do some specific inner work to shift her perceptions of relationships. With every visit I received more and more information on internal adjustments. But this time was different. I was told she was ready now and that her partner was literally next door. She asked me many questions about what he looked like, his occupation and his possible commitments, but I could not see him clearly. (This is often the case and it is usually a sign that an individual should not go looking for a specific person but rather for a type of person exhibiting the necessary traits.) In her case, though, it was repeated to me that he was next door.

'I don't believe you, Heidi,' she answered. 'I have been waiting two years now, and I've made all the inner changes you suggested. My next-door neighbours are happily married, and the other side is an elderly couple. My partner-to-be certainly does not live next door.' When she had finished speaking it was repeated to me that he was next door. I told her again, and stated she must be patient as he was coming soon.

Disgruntled, the woman left. I received an excited phone call from her about six months later. She had indeed met a man she was madly in love with, ten years her senior, at a party the couple next door had thrown three months previously. She said, 'You know what, I almost didn't go. I had been working late and was exhausted. He's completely different from what I normally go for. If I'd met him a few years ago, I wouldn't have been ready for him.' Today, five years on, they are very happily married.

Many good psychics are in touch with reality and are often very 'normal' in looks and attitude. This is often very comforting to people visiting a psychic, as some ideas associated with seers can be alienating. Good psychics are in touch with life, and they have to be. This is because all psychics interpret energy through the filters of their own psyches. If the psyche has a lack of stored information upon which to draw, it is difficult for the psychic to interpret complexities accurately. If there is plenty of knowledge to draw upon, it is much easier for spirits, guides or the higher self to pass a message on.

Good psychics are honest yet kind. They will pass on information that is honest, but they will think about how to deliver an uncomfortable message in a way that you can understand without it causing unnecessary pain. They will think about how to deliver it, depending on the nature of the person receiving. If you are a highly sensitive person or have many fears, they will carefully pass on a message that is life-changing or life-enhancing by using careful language. If you are a person who likes things to be straightforward, they will pass on a challenging message in the way you like to receive it. They will be truthful and honest, detached from any judgement. Poor, average or inexperienced psychics often do not realize that their own issues and judgements get mixed into the pot, and that this can cause them to pass on messages inappropriately.

Speciality

Many great psychics have an area of expertise. Most of those associated with television programmes are mediums whose speciality is the proof of life after death. Others specialize in helping to find missing persons. For some it's predictions of the future; for others it will be relationships, past lives, family issues, weight problems, pets or general emotional challenges that need unravelling. There are still other areas not mentioned, including those who are brilliant at explaining the unseen.

When you are choosing a psychic to attend, it is often helpful for you to have an area in your life for which you would like an explanation. Brilliant psychics rarely do 'general' readings. Their focus will be on a specific area, and they are not interested in proving themselves to you. Often you will also find that they charge a decent amount per hour or for half an hour of their time. This is not because they are 'rip-off merchants', as some may suggest, but because they earn a living from their skill. Often, how confident they are with their skill is reflected in their fees. Most brilliant psychics will give an outline of their services and ask why you desire their service. This is not to gain a huge amount of information from you that they can recite back as a 'message' but to gauge whether they can help you and to use your time together productively. Generally they will not be able to fix your life; they can only help you to formulate a plan based on aspects of your unconscious and the general 'fated' parts which were put in place before you were born.

Maybe this will help: you could compare a brilliant psychic with a financial advisor. A financial advisor would ask questions to see what it is you would like to invest and to see if you are ready. You would not go to a financial advisor with quite a lot of money to invest or when you were flat broke and wanted to find a way of getting out of debt. At the very least, you would go because you wanted advice, and you would be prepared to act on that advice to change your financial position. You could either take everything the financial advisor suggests or choose the parts that work for you and shelve the rest. If the advisor has a fantastic reputation for getting much of it right, you would perhaps be more inclined to take what they say and act upon it.

Similar to the below-average financial advisor, below-average psychics (verging on the deceitful) would be inclined to promise the earth, giving very general information when you are referring to specifics, or claiming areas of energy when there aren't any to read. They will also lack a good reputation and will state a rate that suits you or will allow you to barter. They will also accept people who are defensive and want to see a psychic for a bit of fun. This is because they do not take their skill seriously enough, or perhaps they think it is an easy way to earn money. I do not know a brilliant psychic who will accept rudeness or disrespect for their craft. They will not defend themselves or become argumentative; they will simply say they are not suitable for what the 'client' requires.

How to Find a Brilliant Psychic

Brilliant psychics are often quite a challenge to find, usually because they are very busy or generally keep a low profile. Although they can be hard to locate, there are a few rules that help you to find one.

Personal recommendation has to be the number-one way to find a brilliant psychic. It is also the best way for you to become a client. Brilliant psychics usually have a limited amount of time available and often only take on new clients based on recommendations from clients they already know. If a chosen psychic works well for a friend of yours, then he or she is likely to work well for you. This is because in order for you to be friends with a person you are going to have to share similar energetic vibrations; therefore, you are most likely suitable for the psychic to read, too.

If a personal recommendation is not possible, then choose a psychic by reputation within an area you would like help with. Go for a psychic whose area of expertise is generally in the direction of what you would like to know about. If they cannot help, brilliant psychics will, if they can, recommend you to someone more appropriate for your specific needs.

Websites and forums are good places to look (see Recommended Resources chapter). On many forums discussing psychic matters you will find recommendations for good psychics. With regard to choosing psychics from websites, go with your instinct. If your instinct says they will be great for you, then it is likely they will be. If your chosen psychic proves a disappointment, it is worth your while to review just what it was that you felt drawn to, and ask yourself if you were responding to something superficial, wishful or insincere.

Exhibitions such as mind–body–soul or –spirit events that are sponsored by strongly established organizations will have many excellent psychics in attendance. This is because they are costly to take part in, so only established, confident psychics can comfortably afford to be at such shows. These are different from psychic fairs, which I do not particularly recommend for finding brilliant psychics. If you are generally happy with receiving a reading from someone just starting out, then sometimes you can come across a gem at a psychic fair.

Remember, at any of these types of events, go with your instinct. If there is someone there who you feel is going to be helpful to you, it's likely he or she will be.

How to Become a Brilliant Psychic

There are many people in this world who are naturally very gifted with psychic and mediumship skills. Their gifts may have started spontaneously or be an inherited trait, while for others it is something that has developed over time. A natural skill has its limitations. This is because without strong self-development psychics will generally project their own views, beliefs, limitations and opinions on the information they receive. This does not affect a medium quite so much, since their focus is on proof of afterlife and forwarding messages as they are given.

On many occasions I have witnessed someone with a natural but unchecked talent upsetting people. This generally arises when the psychic practises his or her skills before they are completely developed. One such vivid occasion occurred when a woman with the ability to read energy began to give another woman a reading. The sitter (the person receiving the psychic reading) offered the reader a piece of her jewellery to read. The reader began to receive some very accurate information regarding the sitter's mother, including her character traits, her beliefs and fears, and the sitter's frustrations with her mother. This was all correct information. The reader then became overly confident in her ability to read energy. That was when it all began to go wrong.

The reader started to project her own opinions onto the reading. She said the sitter must behave in a way her mother could accept. She told the sitter how she had lost her own mother without getting a chance to talk to her properly, so the sitter should take the time to say how she was feeling. She then told the sitter her mother was going to die.

Telling a person someone is going to die is highly unprofessional, however true it might be. Such information should be passed on *only* if asked for and the reader is certain it is appropriate for the sitter. In this case, it was not appropriate. The reader, although cautioned, continued to project her reality onto that of the sitter. The sitter would have found information on how to deal with her mother's character much more helpful. She certainly did not need an inaccurate prediction of her mother's demise. This is not responsible in my view, but I have seen it occur many times in people who have a natural skill but have not taken the time first to develop the 'self'.

In order to become an outstanding psychic, then, natural talent is not enough. It is imperative you engage in intensive self-development to conquer any imbalance and to understand your strengths and, even more importantly, your limitations. You must know when to refer something or someone on. Some psychics get very mixed up, believing the information they pass on is without question perfect, and they believe any healing they give is completely accurate. They can get very caught up in their own perceptions and how they have dealt with a similar situation in the past, thereby forgetting how to view it from the perspective of the person they are reading for at that moment.

Brilliant psychics recognize immediately when there is a temptation to do this. They will infuse their way of looking at a situation with open thinking and be able to interpret based on the sitter's reality. They can give the person 100 per cent of their attention when with them, but be able to detach from the outcome of their advice and from the energy of the sitter once he or she has left, no matter how traumatizing the person's story.

The question is, how do you do this?

Self-development

Self-development involves working on the mental aspects of the self, the beliefs structured from childhood experience and life events. It is the process of looking at the 'shadow-self' in order to improve old and outdated beliefs that no longer work or that reflect a reality that is no longer true. It consists of restructuring fear and becoming more aware of how you operate in life. You become able to recognize old behaviour patterns, and you use the opportunity to learn from them. For most people who are new to self-development, knowing what makes you tick is the tricky part and takes much reflection.

Self-development really means becoming aware of who you are and how you think, feel and react, and then taking those features that are based on fear or the ego's need for power and control and changing them into a more wholesome stance that is compatible with others who may feel the same way. It involves realizing that you can change aspects of the self, or inherited behaviours, if you want to. It involves learning new skills for interacting with the world in a way that produces the best results for yourself and for others. Self-development means discarding the excuse 'you can't teach an old dog new tricks' (and its cousin, 'you can't teach a new dog old tricks') – for you certainly can if the dog really wants to learn! Anything can be changed if a person is willing to trust him- or herself and work on it.

Finally, self-development is about bringing aspects of the unconscious mind into the conscious everyday mind, then using various techniques to make it a long-lasting change. It is a linear process that works very well for the logical mind. However, being linear, it is often slow and doesn't necessarily address core issues. Often, people can see where something comes from but feel powerless to change it.

The process of becoming self-aware, however, is an absolutely essential part of becoming a brilliant psychic. It's like kneading dough to make bread. The 'shadow-self' requires much work in order for a person to become accepting of the self or to recognize areas that are not their strong points. This 'working' also develops strong empathy without the need to 'save' another person (what is called 'non-possessive empathy'), and it develops the ability to listen without judgement. All training therapists, from counsellors to psychotherapists, are required to receive therapy themselves for a period of time before they can possibly qualify to counsel others. However, this is not to say self-development is completely fireproof. As with all other aspects of life, self-development carries certain risks, and one risk is the possibility of failure.

Methods of Self-development

It is a shame most people do not seek to change something unless 'what is' becomes unbearable. Many people do not seek to develop themselves until a crisis is upon them and they realize that they absolutely need some assistance in order to move past it. Self-development is not just for a crisis; it is an important part of life. It helps to create inner satisfaction and joy in life by tackling the shadow-self most people spend their entire life trying to hide from.

There are many methods of self-development. A starting point I always recommend is to use a notebook. This notebook is for observing your thoughts and feelings over a period of time, like a week or a month. This helps you to establish what some of your less obvious core beliefs are. Any form of addiction is a great place to start, although for some people the process of even accepting an addictive behaviour can be challenging. Behind most compulsive or addictive behaviours will be an unhappy feeling operating within the shadow-self. Examples can be anything from the obvious, such as alcohol, smoking or drugs, to overspending, overeating, under-eating, underspending, lack of commitment to the self and others, or staying in a relationship that doesn't work. Many of these behaviours will be rooted in a person's sense of self-worth. We all have shadow parts that could use an overhaul. Being perfect would keep us from being human, so having a look at parts of the self that need a bit of work helps you to understand what makes you tick. Knowing yourself is one of the key starting points of developing any aspect of psychic or intuitive awareness.

The second key aspect of self-development for psychic development is to look at what you are frightened of. This can be anything from fear of the dark to fear of relationships.

Looking at what you put off and procrastinate over will also reveal the fear factors behind them, some of which are as yet unacknowledged.

The third key aspect of self-development for psychic development is to go to a large bookshop when you have plenty of time, preferably a couple of hours. Go to the section for popular psychology or self-help. Browse through this section and pick out books that 'speak' to you. Flip through them and buy the ones that feel to you as though they have something for you. If you find yourself resisting going to the bookshop, or you can't find the time, look within for an unexplained fear.

There are some very popular methods of self-development that work for individuals the world over: these include neuro-linguistic programming (NLP), motivational speaking, hypnosis, psychotherapy and many others. I have always had a strong desire to read books and to soak up as many different ways of thinking as I possibly can. My idea of a fun day out is going to a large bookshop with loads of self-development books. Browsing though these types of books, looking for what you are drawn to, will help you to gain a fabulous understanding of this huge arena.

Self-development for psychic development really stops there, and spiritual development then becomes a necessity.

Spiritual Development

Spiritual development is the strongest form of self-improvement towards inner peace and happiness that I have ever seen. Spiritual development involves developing aspects of the psyche from its core. This is most certainly the key to becoming a brilliant psychic.

Spiritual development involves the return of the self to the core aspect of perfection. In our purest form, we are all perfect. The way I look at it, our centre is a bright light beam. Through our lifetime the light beam gets covered up with emotional experiences that leave a negative imprint. These imprints are mixed with the personality and stick to a person depending on how they interpret their experience of the world. Underneath remains the perfect light beam. Spiritual development allows a person to realize that they are this brilliant beam of light and that the muck gathered on top is only temporary. Once we realize this, we then know that the muck on top can be released, as the shining beam radiates through to reveal itself in our eyes. This is why some people look so alive; it is in their eyes.

Sure, if not cleared enough, the muck will build up again, but once a person has experienced spiritual development it becomes a path that is impossible to leave.

Spiritual development is achieved through methods using energy vibrations and frequencies to invoke a release of energy within a person's system that has, until that moment, deepened an untruth. That untruth can be anything from believing you have no confidence to the idea you can't do something. By clearing the muck on top of the metaphorical light beam, a psychic, medium and/or healer will develop abilities beyond imagining. Where previously they have experienced fear or limitation, they perhaps have become stuck. Once 'unstuck', an explosion of development will occur. This explosion will often depend on the person, group or organization leading the exercise. This is because spiritual development is associated with energetic frequencies, so are unique to each individual.

Spiritual development for the beginner involves group work on a regular basis, or directed work from an auditory kit such as a CD or MP3 download. It effects lasting change within a relatively short period of time. Someone once described my particular methods as 'ten years' worth of psychotherapy in ten minutes'. Once a person is willing to enter into the process of spiritual development, a strong inner confidence and peace prevail.

Spiritual development is achieved through guided meditation designed to go into a very deep part of the self and the 'universal consciousness', sometimes described as God or the life source. In most spiritual development designed to assist with psychic development, God or the life source is seen as an energy that connects everything. That energy is the light beam at the core of every person. Some have chosen within their lifetime to tread a life devoid of emotion and morals. This might be due to environmental influences. Sometimes such unsavoury characters can, in spite of themselves, help others to develop in a positive way. Their anti-social behaviours can actually help a person to resolve differences they were not prepared to face previously. Spiritual development helps a person within such circumstances to 'let go and let be'. However, spiritual development is not to be confused with forgiving a person for wrongs; it is releasing the self from the pain such wrongs create, which can eventually develop into ill health after a lifetime of stress.

How Do *You* Empty Your Cupboards?

How quickly an individual develops both spiritually and on a psychic level depends entirely on the person. You may say, 'Well, I want to develop quickly and be able to do *X* by the end of next week.' For some that is a reality; for others it takes much longer. A long time does not mean a person isn't getting anywhere. One woman I know has been to see me for years. Her childhood background was heavily traumatized. Her parents died when she was young, and her formative years were spent in an environment like something in a gothic novel. She lived with an alcoholic uncle and mentally ill aunt who took her inheritance to finance a lavish lifestyle while making the life of the little girl hell.

Not surprisingly, she grew into an alcohol-dependent and very frightened adult, but she also possessed amazing music and singing skills. Over the years I have seen this woman work very hard on herself through spiritual development. She has trusted what I have received and passed on to her, but essentially she has done all the work herself. Of course she is not perfect, but I have to say that she is much nearer perfect than the average individual, for the light of this woman shines brightly. I am immensely proud of her achievements and truly amazed at the tenacity of the human spirit she embodies.

How quickly you will develop your psychic ability or work through the shadow-self and your spiritual development can be assessed using the analogy of how you clean your cupboards out. You have a cupboard full of stuff you haven't looked at for six months or more. Deciding to have a clear-out, are you the type who will look into the cupboard and say, 'No time now, I'll deal with that later.'? Do you take all the stuff out of the cupboard, spend hours going through it and neatly put back three-quarters 'in case I need it later'? Or do you open the cupboard and say, 'I haven't looked at that in at least six months, so I'm unlikely to need anything in there. I don't need to look through it; I know there are no important documents because I keep those elsewhere. I will put the whole lot in the bin.'?

Whichever style you are will reflect how you deal with aspects of the psyche that no longer serve you. If are prepared to sweep things clean without holding on to anything, you will develop very, very quickly on both a spiritual and psychic level. If you put three-quarters of the stuff back, you are going to need to work on learning to trust that clearing something out which you no longer need does not make you less of a person. It makes room for new things, new ideas and the formation of great new beginnings. If you leave the junk in the cupboard, it will take you a long time to develop your psychic gifts, and you will be at risk if you try to use them for other people before you are ready.

Having said all this, spiritual development is a very pleasant journey that can help anyone. For the budding brilliant psychic, it helps you to return to the light beam at your centre, build the 'light body' and access areas of your psyche and the universal consciousness you only ever dreamed of. Spiritual development means a much easier life. Instead of going against the tide you relax into the flow, following the river of life comfortably downstream. Every so often you may hit the odd bump, but generally the flow of the river keeps you moving smoothly along. Everyone else seems to be clambering up the banks or swimming against the tide. Only when they become too tired and give in do they then let go enough to flow with the river. That's why when you are looking for something or are desperately attached to an outcome, it doesn't seem to happen for you. The moment you let go and let be, it all comes at once. Imagine what life would be if you did this every day!

CHAPTER 6
Psychic FM – the Purpose of Readings

What Is the Purpose of a Reading?

The first time I received a psychic reading was at a psychic fair. I walked in nervously, not sure what I would find. I half-expected a scary, overly made-up woman with long fingernails and wearing a purple velvet dress; instead I found myself in front of an elderly woman. As she ate a plate of fish and chips, she proceeded to give me a reading.

People go to see psychics for a variety of reasons, and mine was a deep curiosity. There was something I was fascinated by, yet I did not fully understand what it was. I was looking for an explanation of the psychic occurrences in my life. I wanted someone to make sense of them, especially at a time when such things were far more taboo than they are today. Sitting in front of the elderly woman, I did what most people do on their first visit. I tried to have an open mind, but I couldn't help wondering if this was a sweet little old con artist. It wasn't until, with a mouthful of chips and ketchup, she announced my grandmother was standing behind me, describing her perfectly, that I was convinced I had come across something real and that my own psychic experience was true.

Dilemmas

One of the primary reasons for seeing a psychic in preference to a medium is to have help solving a dilemma. Psychics are not there to fix your life; they are there to give guidance and an open view on 'energy in progress'. Energy in progress simply refers to your life unfolding based on the energy of your past and present mixed with a bit of fate, which together determine your future traits. You could argue that it's nothing but common sense, but I do not know many people who can deliver common-sense meanings including names, places and specific timings.

Unbeknownst to me, the old woman began to decipher and make sense of my biggest dilemma at the time. Should I do something with these psychic senses or ignore them? Wiping her hands, she clasped mine. 'You have the psychic cross in your palm, dear.' *Hmm … what does that mean?*, I wondered. 'It means, dear, you have a great talent. Use and develop that talent. You are young, so there is plenty of time. Your grandmother is there to help you, and she has been sent by spirits.'

For many, such a simple message allows the penny to drop, because what once did not make sense suddenly does. Maybe it's something you have been throwing around in your mind, not sure which path to follow. For me, my doubts, questions and dilemmas had been answered in about ten minutes. These were my private thoughts that perhaps I hadn't been fully conscious of; she brought them out into the daylight for a full airing.

Decisions

I have had many people sit in front of me with important decisions to make. They are often decisions they do not want to discuss with friends or family, perhaps because they fear criticism or rejection from their loved ones. They are usually looking for a neutral view on something important in their lives.

One such woman who came to see me had a decision to make regarding her marriage. For the purpose of this story I shall call her Mavis. She knew she wasn't in love with her husband, but she couldn't make up her mind if a divorce was the 'right' thing. An inner knowledge told her that staying with him would eat away at her, eventually eroding her self-worth; but staying was going to be the 'right' thing because of their four children. Her husband was also unwell, suffering from a long-term, life-threatening illness that was sure to take him within ten years.

This was certainly a tough decision and not one she wanted to discuss with anyone she knew. What would they say? What would they think of her wanting to leave a sick husband and split up the family?

Many people in this world agonize over such decisions but never discuss them with anyone, so in the long term their health suffers through stress. They do their best to remain sprightly while harbouring a terrible secret.

After Mavis had bravely stated her reasons for coming and the decision she wanted to make, I asked her if she really wanted to know what sort of outcome to expect, based on the current energy. I affirmed to her I wasn't there to fix her life, but I could offer a view of the energy as it stood and the likely outcome based on that energy. I told her I often receive, from the sitter's higher self, impressions of what will work to change the energy. Was she sure she wanted to explore the options? She told me she certainly was. I then gave an open, honest account of the energy I could see and where it would take her.

Such a responsible attitude from the sitter enables a psychic to access very high levels of energy and information. This is because such an individual wants help with sorting out the issue.

People like Mavis are committed to their own progress in life and genuinely want to sort something out. Psychics love these sorts of people, and will give them every support they require because they are a pleasure to work with.

I began to view the energy Mavis released. I described what I could feel as her reality – the daily strains she went through, including the agonizing thought processes and the alcohol she was hiding in. Sobbing, Mavis confessed that this was all true. I went on to describe the reality of her husband, how closed off he had become, locked into his work and denying his illness. I also described how, indeed, I could feel most certainly she was not in love with him and never had been. I told her how I felt she had married him because he was safe, as she didn't love him enough to be hurt, so she never would be. Sobbing into a hankie by now, Mavis sat there nodding. I told her that I felt she would be dissolving the marriage and that, in fact, she had already made that decision. I told her that what she had really come for was to find a way of doing it without causing too much pain and suffering. I had a very clear indication she was going to achieve this very successfully. The children would remain happy, her husband would accept it after a period of time, and they would get on fine. I felt his illness would go downhill, then improve as the pressure he had felt himself under to hold the marriage together would change, and he would eventually become a happy man. I reiterated to her that she must only take what resonates as truth and push the rest of what I was saying aside. If parts did not feel 100 per cent right, she had free will to accept my reading or reject it.

At the end of the session Mavis told me a great weight had been lifted. A huge decision suddenly made sense. She told me how long she had kept all this inside her heart, and how she could now let go of feeling shameful.

This is not necessarily how it works out for everyone. Not all readings are clear or easy. People are complex characters with flaws and imperfections, deep denials and internal conflict. For many people, such a decision would be an overwhelming process, and a psychic must respect that. With such skills comes a great responsibility, and all psychics working to a code of ethics will respect that. I had made sure that Mavis was ready to receive answers to such important life changes; if she hadn't been, I would have turned her away.

Mavis continued to see me for a period of time, so I was able to describe to her her husband's feelings and how to handle them. This was not from my opinion; it was through reading his energy, her energy and the energy of the situation. Through respecting at all times how he felt and handling it accordingly, Mavis was able to have a very amicable divorce, remain friends with her ex-husband and allow her children to be relaxed about the whole thing. There were no fights over money, belongings or the children. They were able to handle the inevitable within their relationship in a responsible, adult fashion, setting a good example to their children. It was Mavis who made it all work out, not me. I simply gave her information based on the energy of the two 'main characters', to help Mavis to come to her own conclusions and decisions.

The Skills of a Reading

No medium or psychic is an absolute natural at delivering information; it takes time and experience not only of interpreting information from spirit but also of learning how to handle people. A person who is aggressive or negative and a little hard to handle is intimidating to the most centred of people. To a psychic or medium, such people are like a big, black cloud full of a thick, smoky energy. We can feel their inner world has become entangled in the deepest parts of their denial. This is a hard energy even for the best psychics to work with. It is tiring and intimidating, and for many psychics and mediums their readings in these situations become disjointed, often proving these hardened sceptics 'right' in their judgements. This is why it is vital for the budding, gifted sensitive to learn how to handle the most difficult of individuals. Regardless of whether you choose to use your sixth sense as a skill, if you are a sensitive then you will pick up on the energy of all the people around you. You can feel other people's feelings and thoughts, and often you can find yourself acting them out. Do you sometimes find yourself becoming moody or irritated when five minutes earlier you were fine? If you do, you may have been picking up on the mood of someone passing by.

Calm

Good readings often come from a place of calm. Remember, all psychics and mediums are human beings; they are not a source of entertainment. When a psychic or medium is calm, he or she is able to read information and the energy coming through with much more clarity. When he or she is nervous they make mistakes, like any human being. This is because operating from the personality dilutes the information received, as the personality tries to deal with the normal shortcomings of human nature: am I doing OK? Does this person like me? How can I get them out of this negativity? How can I get them to feel OK with this reading?

Those who have gained experience over a period of time lose their nervousness and are much more able to operate from a calm place. They are capable of helping others to feel at ease, making the sitter more comfortable in their presence.

Certainly, when I am giving someone a reading for the first time I can tell immediately if that person is just nervous and a healthy sceptic or heavy and negative. In my naiveté, I used to try my hardest to impress the heavy and negative people, often wearing myself out and feeling flat for days. Even though I had provided them with some very solid information, it was never enough. Now I choose to work only with the nervous, healthy sceptic who has come for a reason, as well as those who have made progress within their own development and would like guidance from spirit or their higher selves to take it further. I never forget those who have had someone dear to them pass over, who need closure to move forward in their lives.

With this in mind, I am able always to give my best to the person in front of me. All my readings are given from a calm place. As a sensitive, it is important for you to remember that you do not have to help everyone – or anyone, for that matter. It is your choice, and every human being has free will. Certainly, spirits can pressure you, but they can't make your choices for you. Sensitives are always going to be extra-sensitive to their environment and the people in it. It is best that you start to set boundaries and choose what and who will help you to maintain calm in order to pass information of a high quality.

Non-attachment to Outcome

Many people ask me if I become bogged down with the burdens involved with helping people to sort out aspects of their lives. The answer is no, I don't, but I certainly used to. All budding psychics and mediums start with an overly-developed desire to fix lives and protect people from unpleasant outcomes. Over the years I have learned it is part of the richness of life to experience ups and downs, as it is what makes us human. Challenges are there to learn from; and the quicker we learn the lesson, the easier it becomes. The more we hold on to pain and suffering, the longer they last.

The ability to develop non-attachment to outcomes makes it possible for a medium or psychic to give consistently high-grade readings. This is not to say they have to become cold and uncaring. All sensitives are empathetic; that is, they are able to use their skill to understand what a person is experiencing. They can feel what it is like to be that person and have the life challenges they have had. The key is to be able to acknowledge these and feel them, but not keep them. Then the main purpose of the reading becomes apparent, and you must determine how you move these feelings on and what you do based on the reality of the sitter. This is the point at which non-attachment to the outcome is vital in order to relay information as it comes, to avoid bias or incorrect interpretation.

A highly spiritual man came to see me to ask about his relationship. He had fought himself for many years over allowing a relationship to become truly emotionally intimate. Now he saw his current relationship as having the potential for developing into something very deep.

I knew this man well, and I knew the work he had done on himself. I knew that whatever information I received on this relationship he could take and take well. My personality really wanted any information to come through as fully supportive of this relationship, for such a lovely man really deserved happiness. Furthermore, the effort he had put into himself on a spiritual-development level was admirable.

I started to look at the energy of the relationship. I saw immediately in the energy of his partner a wolf in sheep's clothing. I saw her as very pleasant and loving on the surface, and that he would continue to see this side of her for a while. Then, almost overnight I saw that he would see the wolf, a damaged part of her psyche she was unwilling to heal. This was a part of her that had been extremely wounded in her past.

I could feel on a long-term basis the relationship would not and could not last, especially if she was not prepared to heal herself. He was someone who always faced any shadowy parts of himself willingly. I had seen a wonderful man emerge from the ashes of his past by his willingness to face anything uncomfortable. I felt I had no choice but to tell him the relationship had a limited shelf life, and that he would eventually see a part of her that was not in harmony with his loving, nurturing personality.

I passed on the information because I knew he could take it. He had asked for it and, being the spiritual being he is, I knew it was appropriate. For someone else, perhaps I would not have been so honest. I would have toned it down to something they could handle. For example, if I can see or feel someone is about to crash their car I wouldn't say, 'You're going to crash your car!' I would ask if they sometimes drive a little fast. Even if they answered no, I would then say they needed to be a little more steady and careful while driving.

This man took what I said and told me that in his heart he knew I was right, although he was disappointed. All that I had passed on has come to light in recent times.

If I had been attached to the outcome I would have only seen the rosy part at the outset of the reading. I would not have been able to see beyond the honeymoon stage of the relationship. This man thanked me, and through my continued contact with him he was able to give updates on his relationship and enjoy it for what it was: a tremendous learning curve to free him from his past pain, and for her to take the opportunity to do the same if she wanted to. Sadly, this was something she chose not to do. So she remains in her challenges, blaming him for her shortcomings.

Another such example is a woman who continues to use my help. She tells me the reason she asks me for readings is that I am the only person who can see things from a truly honest perspective. A few years ago she called me on a recommendation from a friend of hers to give her some information on a relationship she was in and out of. Tuning in to her, I knew she wanted me to give information she wanted to hear. She wanted everything to be fine in the relationship as she was coming to the end of her possible child-bearing years.

I told her the energy was showing that the relationship was not working out. I told her I was seeing her going through a low period before she would meet someone very special. This man was from abroad, and she would be very happy with him. She would meet him either while he was on a trip here or when she was travelling. I described him as being in a similar profession and a little way off from meeting her. She tried desperately to convince me it was the man she was seeing currently. Detached, I said, 'I'm sorry but it isn't. You asked me a direct question; the direct answer is it isn't him.' Sure, the current man would bounce in and out, but long term he wasn't interested or the right person for her. Disappointed, she put the phone down. I didn't hear from her for a long time. When I did, she admitted to me that she'd found what I'd said hard to take. She then told me I was the only person who was right. She had consulted many psychics on the matter, and all had said her then-partner would come back with open arms. He didn't. She had been happily involved with the man I had described for six months before she got back in touch with me. He was indeed from abroad; he had a similar profession, and she had met him on a plane. He was completely in love with her and was talking of marriage. She was finding it a little difficult to take in, as she now had all that she'd wanted with no effort. She said it took some getting used to, having a man who wanted commitment and knew what he wanted. She thanked me for sticking to what I felt the energy around her was communicating. This was something I could only do through non-attachment to outcome.

Flexibility

Accuracy within a psychic reading often requires an element of flexibility on the part of the reader. Rigidity does not allow for dealing with different mindsets. Energy to be interpreted through the higher self or spirit requires the reader to be able to relate to a variety of issues presented in a way the sitter can understand. Some of these will be spoken by spirit literally, while others are shown through images or metaphors. Some are to be explained as stories so the sitter can relate or understand.

A woman who was going through issues of intense loneliness sat in front of me. Although surrounded by many people in her life, including loving adult children and grandchildren, she felt very much alone in the world. A little perplexed, I didn't know how to help. I was then presented with a strong image of a flock of pigeons. Then I was given specific instruction on how to explain the spiritual significance of this woman's dilemma.

I explained that people were pigeons, for they flock together. Do the things other pigeons do. I then said that I was seeing her as an eagle. I explained that there are far fewer eagles in this world, people who will push themselves above the rabble of the pigeons. I said I could see her flying high above the experience of the pigeons, and she could see from a great height. I said she was highly talented and had been all her life. She had felt herself to be different but could not explain that difference. I told her she was going through a loneliness that all eagles feel at some point in their lives. They feel different because they don't want to do what the pigeons do, but somehow can't or don't know how to fit in. I told her she would meet other eagles.

The heaviness she had been feeling lifted. She could relate very much to the eagle and pigeon story. She had, indeed, had many experiences and achievements throughout her life that most of us only dream of. She had put herself out to change a lot of limited thinking in this world and had achieved it through the very famous documentary films she had made. To this day I have no idea where the pigeon and eagle story came from, but on occasion I am presented with such stories and metaphors to tell. Without flexibility in how I can interpret information, I would not be able to offer stories that people can immediately relate to. Flexibility is a keenness to allow spirits to use my psyche in whichever way they see fit to pass on a piece of information or healing experience that is perfect for the individual sitting before me.

Tarot

Tarot is a set of cards with pictures on them. Each card has a meaning. The cards are shuffled and placed in a spread. The reader then interprets the cards with the sitter in mind.

Tarot reading has a lot of hostile associations. Some people see it as something dark and in tune with black magic. These views have arisen over hundreds of years.

Tarot has a basis in many cultures, but is mainly French in origin. It is believed that Tarot cards were formed by the illiterate population as a game. The game then developed into divination, with some users of the Tarot foretelling future events. This, apparently, was seen by the Church as a means of people developing minds of their own, and was quickly set upon as the devil's work. This view has stuck and continued through many generations.

Tarot, though, simply gives the reader a focus. Of course each card has a general meaning, but the reader must join those meanings together to make sense to the sitter. Tarot is a brilliant way for the novice psychic to allow his or her skills to come to full fruition. This is because the cards give a focus for a wandering mind full of doubt and logic to allow for intuition and sixth-sense ability to shine through. I have given many novice psychics a set of Tarot cards, which they have no clue how to interpret. I have asked them to give a reading. Terrified, they have complied – and ended up pleasantly surprised at how accurate they have been. The secret, I tell them, is to allow the cards to talk. As the confidence of the reader builds, so does their ability to read cards they do not know the logical meaning of.

For anyone with psychic skills or a curiosity within this area of development, I recommend you get the feel of the Tarot. I ask people to get a deck of cards that speaks to them. When you go to choose them, you will know what I mean. Then, get the feel of the energy of the cards and how they communicate with you. After a while the cards will get battered, but you will be surprised at how attached you are to them. For the inexperienced psychic dabbling with his or her skills, Tarot is an excellent way to begin.

Be advised: Tarot cards are a form of energy and should be respected as such. The full deck should be kept together, and if a card is lost the deck must be replaced. For the developing psychic, Tarot cards should be wrapped in a silk cloth and kept in a wooden box. There are many wooden boxes specifically designed to keep Tarot decks in.

When beginning the Tarot, first learn a few basic and simple spreads; this will help you to develop confidence. You will be amazed how a person's psyche will shuffle the cards in exactly the format required for a reading that reflects his or her circumstance.

Tarot works through the unconscious of the person shuffling the cards. The cards will then reflect the reality of the sitter, much as a mirror does. The reader then interprets this reflection as it is now and as it is unfolding. The temptation of the budding psychic is to use the Tarot as a form of prediction for the self. This works to a certain extent if you can remain detached from the outcome. The first spread is the truth, but you will find you have trouble interpreting it unless it says exactly what you want it to say. If it is not what you want, you will find yourself shuffling and shuffling until it gives you the answer you want. This doesn't work! Get someone else to do your reading! However, once you have mastered how the Tarot works for you, then use it for your own circumstances – providing you are willing to read the interpretation objectively.

Photographs

Reading photographs is one of the easiest forms of psychic ability to master. This is because you have a static image of a person to work from rather than having to work through all your own issues, fears and limitations first. In all the classes and workshops I have taught over the years, the clairvoyance-from-photographs section never ceases to amaze people with how well they do.

People are placed into pairs. Each member of a pair does not know the other. I do this because it helps people to realize that their skill is real. They soon realize that they are not relying on some sort of background knowledge. Each person has a set of photographs of people they know well, preferably close friends and family so they can verify the information easily. Within their pairs, they swap photographs. I give each pair a set of areas to focus on, tell them the types of information to go for first as a way in, and then to allow the rest to flow.

People who previously believed they had no psychic ability find themselves able to pass on accurate information regarding the people in the photographs. Some of this relates to their character but mostly to how their life is, how it has been, and how it is panning out. They are able to achieve this through initially achieving focus. I then show people how to shape and use that focus. It is my belief that everyone is psychic; we all have the innate skill to use a natural part of our life energy for the benefit of both 'self' and 'others'. And that ability *is* the sixth sense.

Psychometry

Psychometry is holding an object belonging to another person for the purpose of reading the energy contained within that object. The easiest form of psychometry involves holding an item of jewellery from the person receiving the reading. This is because metal holds energy well. From this item it is possible to pick up on the character, inner world and motivations of the person to whom the item belongs. In classes and workshops, I stand outside the room gathering items of jewellery belonging to each attendee. I put all the items in a basket and place it in the centre of the room. Each attendee chooses an item out of the basket. They have no idea whose jewellery they have; this prevents the logical mind from ruining the experience. I run through a series of techniques on how to read the psychic information stored in the item of jewellery without giving too much information away on what to expect. Again, this prevents the logical mind from believing it has been *told* what to do.

I ask each person in the group to speak when they have something, no matter how trivial they believe it to be. Many things that are irrelevant to one person can mean a tremendous amount to another. It also prevents build-up of a block. I am careful to tell the group that it doesn't matter if they get it wrong; we're not perfect and practice makes perfect. Only at the end of the exercise can people speak or admit any information given as correct. This prevents the psyche from forming a predetermined view of what type of information 'should' relate to the person based on his or her appearance.

In one class a woman held up a ring. It wasn't obvious as to whether this was a man's or woman's ring. It was fairly chunky, but both genders can wear chunky jewellery. The woman started to get images of a ballet dancer and great joy associated with dancing. She went on to disclose other information regarding the dancing and other aspects of this person's life. When asked, she said she believed the jewellery belonged to a ballet dancer.

At the end of the exercise, the person to whom the ring belonged was asked to collect it. It turned out to belong to a man in his sixties. The woman told him she was sorry and disappointed she hadn't got anything right, for she thought that he obviously wasn't a ballet dancer. This was quite wrong on her part, however: he had been a ballet dancer as a young man, and he'd enjoyed his dancing immensely. He went on to tell her that every piece of information she'd given had indeed been correct.

If on her first occasion of doing psychometry I had placed her in front of this man, she would have discounted the information as incorrect because the images she was receiving would not have matched her preconceptions about him. This is human nature, but the budding psychic or medium always, at some point, must master it.

CHAPTER 7
Psychic Chakras – the Energetic Dustbins

The chakras are an important, if not vital, part of psychic development. The chakras are energy points throughout the body. *Chakra* is a Sanskrit word meaning 'wheel'; each energetic point is shaped like a wheel. The chakras are invisible to the naked eye and exist as energy points at a slight distance from the physical body. Although you are not able to see the chakras, you will know of their existence: each time you have felt a lump in your throat, butterflies in your stomach or a gut feeling, you have experienced the motions of the chakras.

Within psychic development, the importance of the chakras is based upon the necessity for a balanced, centred self. No matter how strong your natural skills of mediumship or psychic ability are, without a balanced, strong centre the skill will eventually drain or frighten you. This is because all those with a heightened natural psychic gift or sensitivity will have faster-moving chakras than the average Joe.

These energy points gather, maintain and build upon your ability to process energy and information regarding any second sight. The faster the energy points begin to move, the more access you will find yourself gaining within the psychic and spiritual realms. Challenges arise if you are not ready for this heightened activity because your system is out of balance. If this is the case, you may find yourself within the undesirable aspects of the spiritual realms. This is what people interpret as the 'dark side'. I shall explain more of what this means in relation to the chakras later on.

I like to relate a person's psychic and medium skills to that of sand in a test tube. The more sand there is in the tube, the more difficult it is for spirits to communicate with an individual. The messages get mixed up as it becomes a challenge to hear. The same is true of psychic skills. When trying to read a person's energy or to listen to the higher self, if your tube is full of sand, then much of what you think is correct in relation to the other person could be projections from your own psyche. This is where inaccuracies come from.

Clearing the chakras means bringing them into a state of balance. Clearing the sand in the tubes allows for clearer communication from spirits to the higher self and the ability to 'hear' your soul frequency. This helps to lead a person to fulfil a sense of purpose and belonging in this world, fine-tuning his or her skills without fear of rejection from others.

Energetic Dustbins

Each of the seven main chakras is an energetic power point, but collectively they are also dustbins for all the thoughts and feelings you have. All lower-frequency energies end up in one of the main seven chakras to be processed out. As you can imagine, over a lifetime emotions stockpile until the dustbins can get pretty full. Each event that has ever frightened you builds up until eventually a phobia develops, with the pounding of your chest during a panic attack or the butterflies doing a clog dance in your belly. These build into irrational fears, anxiety and a lack of trust. These fears may not be entirely conscious, but they do dictate aspects of our behaviour and choices. All these are symptoms of a full, stinking dustbin. By emptying the dustbins every so often, nothing is allowed to build up. This is why many people who choose to develop the spiritual and psychic side of their nature lose their old fears and begin to establish a strong inner confidence and trust. In the meantime their psychic, intuitive or mediumship skills go through the roof!

Emptying the Dustbins

Emptying the bins takes time and, as with the bins in your kitchen, is not a one-time operation. No one has balanced chakras 100 per cent of the time. We all have messy systems that get out of kilter. Those who actively acknowledge this and work on their energy system have a much better ability to keep any imbalances in check.

So how do you empty the bins? This depends on your nature and whether you notice when they are full. Most people have no real idea of their stress levels or when something needs adjusting. Most of us wait until something or someone falls over before changing an aspect of our lives that requires adjustment. Learning how to recognize when something goes against our deepest grain and having the courage to change it depend on our ability to know what goes on in our own body. To do this you must learn to match the communication between your 'head' and your 'heart'. That requires listening to your body rather than relying on the logical thought processes of your head.

This is best achieved through *release work*. Release work involves releasing the stored energy of old emotions in the body. This is the core aspect of emptying those bins. This can be achieved by listening deeply to yourself, the lies you tell yourself, the quiet chatter that dictates how you operate in this world.

These are the 'I'm jealous, I'm not worthy, I'm not enough,' parts of you. Listen to what they have to say and how they restrict your choices. Take notice of where you feel them in your body. We all have them, no matter how balanced we think we are.

Let the feeling roll up to the surface within the stored chakra. You will feel it if you listen. Imagine that feeling as a pencil in your hand. Let the feeling build, as though you were clasping that pencil tightly. Open the imaginary palm and let the pencil roll out onto the floor. You have just emptied a bin.

In some of the classes I teach, and especially in the talks and demonstrations I give across the UK, I use a powerful guided meditation to empty the dustbins. It involves going through each of the seven main chakras and pushing out the debris. Immediately afterwards people feel very light and airy. A man I took through this process, after years of busying himself through various means of self-development, finally had an amazing breakthrough simply by emptying his bins.

Feel the Fear

In my experience, feeling what you are afraid of immediately empties a dustbin. I know that many teachings and processes encourage a person to step over their fears and rise above them. In what I have seen over the years in the healing work I have done, I notice that having the courage to feel and go deeply into a fear causes it to pass through very quickly. This is because the fear is then properly acknowledged in the conscious awareness in terms of the body as well as the mind. The energy is released in the part of the body where it is stored, usually in one of the seven main chakras.

Sometimes it is not possible for a person to do this alone. Often the assistance of a healer is required in order to lift the energy enough to allow the low-frequency energies to break free. Again, a person can feel much lighter and free of the restriction of the lower-grade energies they no longer need. The rotted food is finally emptied from the dustbin.

The Seven Chakras

The Base Chakras: Vital for Balance

The base chakra is positioned at the bottom of the spine. It is the chakra that processes survival issues, from what makes you get up in the morning to fears of over-providing for the self and others. Its traditional colour is red; it is the root of who we are.

For balance, in terms of psychic development the base chakra is extremely important. Being the chakra that is felt least, often people are particularly unaware if this part is off-centre. It is so important because the energy of the base is about being present in the here and now. For many psychics and mediums, there is a daily struggle to remain grounded. Those who properly harness their psychic and intuitive skills are very real. They are superbly in the here and now; you wouldn't imagine them as anything different. Those who are distracted and out of balance have tremendous difficulty with feeling safe in the world and often have great difficulty with managing their finances. Most are broke and really struggle to take care of their most basic needs. The base chakra, therefore, is critically important in managing your ability to be fully present.

The Sacral Chakra: Great for Psychic Awareness

The sacral chakra is orange. It is about creativity and our ability to use this aspect of the self in our enjoyment of life. It is positioned around the area of the navel. Creativity and psychic awareness are very closely linked. It is said that the psyche uses a very similar area of the brain for imagination as it does for the intuitive senses. All the greatest artists, writers and inventors have relied upon their inspiration and intuitive senses to create monumental works that have survived for generations.

All those who have a heightened sense of psychic skills are able to use their creativity well. This may show in all aspects of their lives, or it may emerge in a limited arena. Easy flow through the sacral chakra is a vital component to a balanced, highly developed system. Exercise, especially yoga (see pages 155–156), keeps the sacral area flowing beautifully and is certainly very important for anyone with a naturally high psychic awareness. This is because the energy needs an output. If it is not used, it collects in the abdomen. This can then turn into a health issue, which is why you see a lot of psychics with too much weight around the middle; it isn't always due to over-indulgence!

The Solar Plexus Chakra and Strength

Gut feelings sum up the area of the solar plexus, and it is yellow, the colour of the sun. In terms of psychic development, the solar plexus is the centre of the mind. Most people think the mind is positioned in the head; however, while using the solar plexus within psychic skills the 'mind' is situated within the energy of the solar plexus. The solar plexus is the power centre, and information in terms of a 'feeling' comes through this energetic area. It is important to work on your own fear issues in order to balance this area and minimize any mix-up with what you are filtering in terms of higher-source information with that of the lower self, or personality.

The Heart Centre Chakra and Love

The heart chakra is positioned in the centre of the chest. It is bright green, although some like to refer to it as pink. In traditional terms the heart centre has to do with matters of the heart, such as love. Most people developing their psychic skills, whether intentionally or spontaneously, go through a period of time when the heart centre wishes to balance. When the heart centre is going through its own clearing process, it can feel like a pulling and tugging in the centre of the chest. In rare circumstances or during a time of an intense release of an energy that is no longer required, the heart centre can feel really quite painful. A deep pain you cannot really explain in physical terms sears from somewhere deep in the centre of the chest. The reason the heart centre tends to 'heal' itself, whether you like it or not, is because it relates to worth and self-esteem through the emotion of love towards the self.

Psychic skills, no matter how developed your natural talent, are not productive or sustainable if there is no love for the self. No one can truly love or feel empathy for another without first developing love for the self. Love for the self is shown through a deep self-respect and honouring personal boundaries and learning when to say 'no'. A lot of people, especially women for some reason, have to unlearn always putting others before self.

Of course, when done in moderation, putting others first is an unselfish act, but doing so all the time is martyrdom. Martyrdom in terms of medium and psychic ability has a limited shelf life, although many go through a period of time with a strong inclination towards this energy. Once your energy system has had enough of its energetic boundaries being forever violated, it will force your system into balance.

For some this is particularly painful, as deep-rooted barriers start to emerge and the energy breaks up to establish balance. This can manifest as a period of time where you go through many tears. The tears last for a short period before everything is absolutely fine again. It is what we might call 'clearing', and it is a normal and natural act. It is important to remember that the changes created by a heart centre energy balance have no commonalities with clinical depression symptoms.

The Throat Chakra and Expression

A deep blue, the throat chakra is, fairly obviously, positioned at the throat. The times you would have been the most aware of the throat chakra energy are when you have a 'lump' in your throat. For psychic development, the throat chakra is essential for a full and clear expression of energy during interpretation through the psychic senses. In everyday life, the throat chakra is responsible for clear expression and speaking your truth. If, when divulging a message, the throat chakra of the messenger is blocked, the message will often become disjointed, vague and unclear. A balanced throat chakra speaks honestly. The honesty is presented kindly with no malice attached. Nothing sticks in a balanced throat chakra; words are expressed truthfully and effortlessly.

For many people the throat chakra is an area requiring strong balance, especially for those who perhaps had a stifled childhood where full expression was either not permitted or was unsafe through the threat of physical or emotional harm.

How the Third Eye Chakra Operates the Sixth Sense

The third eye, or 'brow chakra', is positioned in the centre of the forehead and is often seen as lilac. It is the intuitive centre where, together with the energy of the solar plexus, psychic information is filtered. For most mediums, the third eye is how they use their ability to communicate with the other side. For psychic information, the third eye is used in conjunction with the solar plexus. The solar plexus confirms the energy received through the third eye.

The third eye is used for converting energy into a series of images used for mediumship and any form of clairvoyance. When this area is going through a strong opening process, it can feel like a dull, pulling sensation stretching across the centre of the forehead. People going through a strong opening of the third eye also tend to want to get any hair away from the face or are constantly rubbing the centre of their forehead. This is because, as the third eye energy opens up, it wants to stretch to 'see'.

As an interesting aside, Hinduism has a long tradition of meditation. Much of the Hindu tradition stresses focusing the attention on the 'third eye', or brow chakra, when in a meditative state, and this spot also goes by the name 'Star of the East'. When viewed from this perspective, the idea of the three Magi in the story of the birth of Christ takes on a whole new meaning. Instead of seeing an astronomical phenomenon, it is quite possible that the three wise men were following a spiritual vision.

The Crown Chakra and Connection to Life

The brilliant white crown chakra is positioned on the top of the head. The energy of the crown connects you to life and all living things of the past and present. It is your connection to whatever you term as the life force, God, Mother Nature, the Source or whatever is your chosen word to describe this unquestionable energy. For you to be interested in reading this, your crown chakra will be nicely balanced. As it stretches further and deepens your connection to life, it can feel as though someone is gently playing with your hair. There is a gentle 'tickling' feeling that passes over the scalp.

Issues Associated with the Chakras

It is important to remember the energy of the chakra system is a complex, multi-layered system. The points brought to light in the above section only touch on the areas associated with the chakras. Ultimately they are an energetic entry point for a person to deal with many aspects of their life. I have seen over the years how people have worked on these vital parts of the self to move through tremendous challenges. The chakras deal with physical, emotional and mental issues, and anything dealt with in these important centres transforms the apparently immovable.

A woman whom I have known for years went to see a specialist after experiencing strong stomach pains, fatigue and generally low energy. After tests, she was diagnosed with cancer. The tumour was large, and X-rays showed that it had spread from the womb to the stomach wall.

Shortly before she was due to go for surgery, she asked me to look at the cancer from an energetic standpoint through the chakra system. I became aware of an energy trapped between the sacral area and the solar plexus. In my mind I saw tremendous grief and a man. I then felt the energy of the cancer symbolized by a dead baby, and I felt the energy was about ten years old.

It happened that this woman had lost her partner ten years previously, and her biggest regret was she hadn't conceived a child with him. I asked her if she had wanted to 'die' ten years ago. She confirmed she had wanted to die then, but truly wanted to live now. I asked her again if she wanted to live. She said she definitely did want to. I then felt a strong energy release in her system, which she felt also.

A couple of days later the surgeon opened her up to remove the tumour, which had been very apparent in her previous scans. A 'spontaneous healing' had occurred; the tumour was no longer there. The signs it had been there were evident. He had to put her insides back in their correct order as the tumour had squashed many of the major organs out of their intended position. Closing her up, he said to her later that he was amazed the tumour had disappeared.

Concerned over the amount of fluid still present, he was convinced that the cancer must have spread. Terrified while waiting for her final results, she asked me if I thought there was any more cancer in her body. I told her I couldn't feel any and that the fluid was harmless. A couple of weeks later her surgeon was able to confirm this, and six years later she remains cancer-free.

What I helped this woman to do was not a miracle cure on my part. I simply highlighted an energy occurring within her chakra system. Her truth allowed her body to release enough energy to create the spontaneous healing. In other cases it is not part of a person's pathway to heal the self to that extent, but such a story shows that, in some circumstances, it is possible.

How to Strengthen the Chakras for Psychic Development

There are many very simple ways you can strengthen and balance your chakras. Meditation is an important part of psychic development, certainly in the early days. It encourages a disciplined and quiet mind, a 'library', where you can be open to hearing communication from spirit and the higher mind.

Spending time outside in nature helps any imbalances. It is also a vital aspect of remaining grounded. On a very basic level, going for a walk in the woods or in an open space calms the most stressed of individuals, whether they have psychic skills or not. Thus you can see how something so easy can make a huge difference.

Healing or any form of energy work, including massage, will encourage stagnant energies to leave the chakra system. It is important to use an energy worker you are comfortable with or you have been recommended to. Your energy system needs to relax for a deep release, and if you are uncomfortable with the person facilitating that release, then your system will not open up enough.

Cold showers in winter sound like an awful idea! Unfortunately, they work at any time of the year. A brief, three-second flash of a cold shower over your head will shock the energy system, forcing out anything that has collected during the day, or that was on its way out. If you are prone to picking up on the thoughts and feelings of others, especially their fears, a cold shower is a must.

Finally, but not exclusively, an Epsom salts bath will help to even out the chakra system and encourage a dustbin emptying. Epsom salts are available from pharmacies and usually come in a large bag. Simply tip a few tablespoons of the salts into a warm bath before stepping in. Afterwards, your energetic sphere will feel refreshed and renewed.

CHAPTER 8
Blocks to Psychic Awareness

Many people ask me what the possible blocks to psychic awareness are. Some make comments about an interest in psychic awareness but feel as though they have no psychic power at all. Others seem to know they have a psychic awareness but currently feel blocked or like they have reached their limit of psychic development. One of the key aspects to psychic awareness is to embrace rather than avoid an open curiosity and fascination with human life. Therefore, two of the main blocks are avoidance and denial. If you try to hide from your life, determining there must be a bogey-man the size of an elephant in your cupboard, then psychic awareness is not going to be easy for you no matter what your natural gift.

Believe me, no one has anything in his cupboard he cannot face. Faith and trust are all that is required. Many of the most sensitive and psychic individuals walking the planet have not had an easy start, either physically or emotionally. You may argue that some people do have drastic things to avoid and bury deep in the psyche, never having the courage to face. The answer is, facing them with trust in the self will get a person positive results every time. I have seen people come out the other side of childhood rape, being left for dead after an attack, brutal domestic violence and many other extreme traumas at the hands of people without conscience. For some it has taken them years to overcome the damage, but they have done it successfully. Often it has been as a direct result of their trust and willingness to face the unseen shadow part of the self and moving through it by using energy work on the 'spiritual field', rather than talking it through the 'mental field' of psychiatric care. This is not to say that psychiatric care or psychotherapy is ineffective; it has its place, and it works for many. But even the best psychotherapy will fail if the individual doesn't do the self-improvement work that also leads towards psychic awareness.

The Importance of Meditation

At the start of my psychic path I had a strong desire to reduce fats, sugars and caffeine in my diet, and I even developed a food allergy that I can only describe as a blessing. It gave me the ability to focus on the simple things in life and clear the clutter of old thoughts and feelings. As mentioned earlier, if the mind is quiet we can 'hear' more clearly. If we have a party in our head, then our feelings cannot be heard, and spirits have no chance of getting through.

Many people don't know a lot about meditation, and many more have powerful critical judgements about it. It sounds vaguely alien and 'Eastern', not like something practical people should bother with. But the fact is that everyone already meditates. That moment or two at night between the time you are awake and asleep is meditation. But it's a form of meditation that is brief, undisciplined and usually unproductive (although you may have noticed that there are times when you come up with important insights or solutions to vexing problems just as you're falling off to sleep). For psychic development, meditation must be pursued as a discipline.

A block for many people is that they have a mind far too busy for easy communication from the higher self or from spirits. This is especially true in the early days, or when the communication received is confusing. Confusion depletes confidence; it is perhaps that a person's life has become stressed or chaotic, and the information received through psychic channels reflects that. Perhaps the once-clear messages become misty and vague. This is often because in the early days the individual did not focus on or master meditation.

Meditation is not about sitting cross-legged and bored in silence. It is a process of opening up the mind and teaching it to be more disciplined. A disciplined mind deciphers information clearly and is less likely to fall into the trap of projection. It can interpret the often subtle differences between imagined thought and true psychic communication. Meditation is also an easy way to clear the debris cluttering the mechanisms of the intuitive thought processes.

Meditation can be practised in a number of ways. For the beginner it is best to use guided meditations at first because they are an easier way to get into the psyche. Instead of staring at the blank slate of your mind and wondering what to do next, a guide can help you through the initial relaxation and then into a state of 'thoughtlessness' that is the real threshold of true meditation. This is possible to do at home using quiet time. Around bedtime or early morning is usually the most convenient time. Meditation has the added bonus that it can help dramatically with getting a restful night's sleep, and helps to create a clear day with a peaceful mind. Here's a tip, though: If you start to meditate and you fall asleep, you're still at the beginning stage of mastery. The idea is to go to sleep *after you've finished* meditating.

For those not used to it, ten minutes is the recommended maximum amount of time. If boredom creeps in, take it as a sign of an undisciplined mind at the beginning of training. Practise often. At first your mind will probably race, or you will have trouble with the imagery suggested in the meditation. You might find yourself 'disappearing' until you are instructed to return to the room, or you may even fall asleep. This is nothing to worry about; your psyche will still hear and take in the information. The deepest part of you may need to 'disappear' in order to rejuvenate, especially if you've had a busy or worrying time. Sleep is often a way for the psyche to empty the filing cabinets anyway, so meditation in this sense quickens the pace of this clear-out as the psyche gets a helper.

The relaxation meditation I use at the beginning of every class I teach, available on my website as a free download, helps people, at the very least, to let go of their day (see Recommended Resources). This makes opening up the senses for psychic development very easy. A woman who comes to my classes often comes almost solely for the relaxation. She says she now has the best sleep in years and feels much more relaxed in her everyday life. It is a simple and easy mediation to follow, with accompanying sounds that help to slow down the brainwaves. Anyone who wants to start meditating can do it.

Logical Mind

What really helped to accelerate my own psychic ability was my constant curiosity and willingness to abandon fear and contain the 'logical mind'. I saw every challenge as an opportunity to discover something new, and I found that when I crossed a bridge in life my psychic ability strengthened. My 'logical mind' was often working overtime. It would squeak at me about making things up and having a vivid imagination. Rather than believe it, I observed these thoughts as something distant from me, although always respecting the logical thoughts as part of a necessary function of life. Now I can easily discern the psychic information I receive, sifting through which bits are correct and which bits could be interpreted as the products of an overactive imagination.

The logical mind is a powerful and necessary part of the psyche. In psychic development it helps us to remain grounded and realistic. In life it helps us to determine fact from fiction and distinguish between what is real and what is imagined.

However, on the flipside the logical mind does impose restrictions and keeps us in the confines of thinking that what we see is the only thing that's real. If we believed this in its truest form, then electricity would not be such an important part of our lives. We cannot see how this 'energy' of an electric force pushes into the lamp or light fitting, but we see a very necessary end result.

Our logical mind takes us along a linear pattern of thinking. Logically, one thing follows another. If we want to go from London to Brighton without a car, logically we would look at the train timetable. The next part of the journey is to get on the train and arrive in Brighton. This is fine, and gets us to our destination.

If logic were put aside we might still decide to go from London to Brighton, but our pattern of thinking would be different. The journey may again involve arriving in Brighton without a car, but this time we would think in circles. If you are thinking in circles, then your options become wider. Standing metaphorically in the centre of the circle every option has equal validity, but we can see all the options more clearly. Perhaps we want to get to Brighton without spending the money on a train fare, but we do not want to hitch-hike. Thinking in circles may help us to see other possibilities. Asking at work if anyone is going to Brighton may turn up a friend who happens to be going and who offers a lift, or you find out there's a coach offering a deal straight to Brighton town centre. Such options would not be available to us if we were locked into thinking in only one way. Likewise, an overemphasis on logical thought and scepticism will slow your progress in psychic development. This is not to say everything you hear should be believed, but if logical thought takes over completely, then opportunities are missed.

The typical occasions when I have seen the drawbacks of the logical mind are when I talk to someone about their progress with their psychic skills. I often come across comments like, 'If only I could trust what I get. Often it's true, but I don't know when to tell the difference.' The difference is an open view, as even the most experienced psychics wrestle with their logical mind. Group environments in which to practise help to ease any challenges with trusting the information you receive through the psychic channels, as this information can be tested against past truths.

If you are struggling with your logical mind, the best option is to put it to one side, even for a moment. Experiment with your day. See what it feels like to put your 'logical stamp' in a drawer for a while. Begin to feel the opportunities and the flowering of your thoughts as they open up to a new side of your creativity. Your intuition will grow beyond what you ever imagined.

People Are Different

Sometimes blocks can be due to individual differences. Not everyone is the same. Unique qualities affect how quickly a person can open up his intuitive side. This is often very simple and you find that your intuitive progress steams forward dramatically. The adjustment that comes is to a person's self-worth. Most people's self-worth could do with a boost.

Very often when a person is working on this part of himself, there is a natural progression into the intuitive side. Intuition naturally increases the more self-worth a person has. This is not to say that people with high self-worth are the ones who are the most psychic, because some become aware of their interest or ability in the psychic and spiritual realms following a crisis or dramatic life change that may have affected their self-esteem negatively.

All the courses I teach are centred on people gaining confidence in their intuitive and psychic skills. This is achieved through subtly improving people's energetic worth. They feel this as an increased inner calm and confidence. The high-strung become calm, and the quiet people become more expressive. If someone has hit a wall in their intuitive ability or if they feel stuck, I have found tackling a self-worth dilemma always moves them forward.

It is important to remember the uniqueness of every person. How quickly your intuitive ability opens up will depend on whether you are a hare or a tortoise. If you are a tortoise and you attempt to develop at the hare's pace, you will come unstuck. There is such a thing as going too fast, and if you do go too fast it will tend to show up as overwhelming feelings of fear. I have seen people trying to hurtle along to some sort of destination rather than enjoying the journey. In the process they have opened up too fast and frightened themselves. Dark energy, real or imagined, on occasion can become part of their experience. For some this dark energy resembles what they imagine to be a devil. When this happens to people it is their imagination at work, not the reality of the spirit plane of existence. Energy, due to the unsettled nature of their psyches, collects and manifests itself as their perception of evil. It is a reflection of fears and deep levels of the unconscious, otherwise known as the 'shadow' side of a person's psyche. This is easily rectified, but it is still frightening to those who have no explanation of it.

Some 'hares' are able to progress on a psychic level at the speed of lightning. When this occurs it is described as a profound natural talent, but it will still, of course, have its limitations if not managed and settled to some extent.

Over-cautious and Negative Thinking

It is possible to be overly cautious within the realm of psychic development. Perhaps this is because of fear or preconceived ideas; whatever the source, it can inhibit psychic development. For some this may show up as a habit of negative thinking or seeing the worst in situations. This will inhibit your ability to tap into the whirlpool of resources deep within your psyche.

Negative thinking indulges the logical mind in its most abhorrent form. The psychic antenna becomes dysfunctional, and any true intuitive resources get bogged down in the fog. That is why it is difficult for people to discern correctly when they are not in the right frame of mind. Thinking positively is easier said than done for many people, especially when they see the world conspiring against them. The way to settle this takes effort. Consistent negative thinking is a clear indication of an undisciplined mind or one that is temporarily running wild. Keeping it in check will bring forward the intuitive mind and peace within the psyche.

If you are troubled by consistent negative thinking, observe it as behaviour from a childish part of your psyche. This will help to reduce its effects. Viewing the negative part of the psyche as something separate helps you to move on from getting caught up in the detail of an argument or disagreement and to keep your energy field strong. 'He said / she said' doesn't get you anywhere. Viewing the behaviour as separate from you will.

Quietening the mind into disciplined thinking through balancing the male and female energies within will also have a fantastic effect, taking you into an instantly quiet space. Most people have lives filled with things to do. Much of what we actually do is minimal compared to the mind's chatter. Frustration chirps up, followed by a busy, irritated mind. This will instantly block psychic awareness. Regardless of gender, everyone has both male and female energy, also referred to as *yin* and *yang*. Allowing the male and female energy to remain in an uneven state will create negative thinking and a busy head. An imbalance will also reflect negatively on interpersonal relationships in your life. If you have someone in your life who is a constant 'pain in the neck', this will be a reflection of the imbalance in the male and female energies. Balancing the male and female energies is one of my favourite classes to teach, and it never ceases to amaze me the difference people feel after this simple exercise and the insight they gain into their own psyches. The details of how to balance the male and female energies are inappropriate to explain here, but they can be found in my home-study and course information.

CHAPTER 9
Clairvoyance and Mediumship

There is quite a stark distinction between clairvoyance and mediumship, one that needs to be observed if you are to be clear on your particular or potential skill. Clairvoyance refers to those who have the ability to 'see clearly'. It is the ability to pass on information from a precognition perspective; that is, the ability to see the future before it happens. This is obviously very helpful for seeing round corners, so to speak, but it is also disconcerting for those who don't like what they see.

Some natural clairvoyants are also mediums. Mediums act as a bridge between this world and the spirit world. Those who are mediums as well as clairvoyants have the ability to talk to spirits, plus they can gain an idea of future trends as far as a person or situation is concerned.

Psychic protection is necessary for both of these skills, especially in the early days.

Psychic Protection

Psychic protection is a method of protecting the energy field of a person from outside influences. Going through the 'opening' process in the early days can leave one's energy field vulnerable.

I like to describe the beginning of the psychic path as similar to collecting lanterns. When you step onto the path, lanterns are placed along your way. Some of these lanterns are easy to find, but others you have to climb up to get, or they are positioned awkwardly. As you start to collect lanterns, other people like to try to borrow or steal them from you. If you have collected only one or two lanterns, you are going to notice if one has been taken. Your energy might dip around certain people or situations. Most people can think of the places or people that make them feel 'yuk'. The 'yuk' feeling arrives because your lanterns are being used, often without your permission. Those people have borrowed or stolen your lantern – that is, your energy. You will also be doing this at times to others without realizing it. This is why psychic protection is needed.

When you have collected quite a few lanterns, say 20 or so, you're not going to notice if a couple are taken. A couple of lanterns disappearing, once you have plenty, is not going to make any difference; hence, once you are more familiar with building your light, it isn't necessary to think about psychic protection. But if lots are starting to disappear, at some point you will say, 'Excuse me. I'll have some of those back, please!'

Methods of Psychic Protection

If you find someone is stealing your lanterns, there are many methods to protect your energetic field. The main one is to remain in a positive frame of mind. Resentment towards others or situations creates psychic attack. Imagine what it feels like when you are on the receiving end of resentment, especially if you are sensitive enough to pick it up. The jagged ends to the energy create pressure on your field. Feeling resentment or anger towards a person puts a huge pressure on their field, but more importantly it will eventually bounce back to your field.

A woman once asked me to help her with a delicate situation. She was a senior manager in a hospital. She had been given the unpleasant task of dismissing a nurse. The managers immediately above the nurse were too frightened to approach the woman themselves. This nurse had been practising voodoo magic on patients. Whole wards were terrified, including the staff.

The senior manager who came to me for help was desperate. I had no knowledge of voodoo, so I had little to work with. I used one of the simplest yet most powerful methods of psychic protection. I redirected the energy the nurse was sending out back to her from afar. Within a day I received a phone call from the senior manager to say she'd had no need to approach the woman to dismiss her. She had very suddenly appeared extremely frightened; her leaving was described as her throwing a resignation letter and running off. Whether or not I had anything much to do with it, the apparent response of the nurse shows how being careful of what you send out is important, particularly the more capable or sensitive you are to the sixth sense.

Releasing resentment can be easier said than done. Allowing yourself to feel the emotion and to ask in your mind what it is the other person is reflecting in you will help to disperse the resentment. Failing that, receiving healing that is particularly specialized towards the emotions will most certainly release it.

There are some basic methods of psychic protection on an everyday level. The most effective has been mentioned earlier and is not the most pleasant, particularly in the winter months: a brief cold shower. Three seconds of cold water on your head will shock any gathered bits of debris out of your energy field.

Clearing your life up also helps to keep your energy field free of any 'sticky' parts. This includes clearing out spare rooms, the magazines and papers stacked up in the corner of your living room, and the things you haven't looked at in months or years gathered in drawers and in the loft or garage. In clearing these things up you are walking into a clear energy when you get to the safety of your own home at night.

Mediums/Mediumship

Mediumship is the receipt of information not available through the normal senses. The information typically comes from the 'spirits' of the dead. Mediums serve as a bridge or channel for communication between the living and the dead. They relay information and act as go-betweens. Some mediums also pass healing energy through their systems in order to help people on this side and on the other during a reading. A medium's communication with spirit is often governed by entities known as spirit guides. Spirit guides can sometimes actually be an extension of the medium.

Mediumship typically manifests in adult years, but early signs are prolific in childhood. A child hearing or seeing things that others do not is a sign of later possibilities of a natural gift. However, if a medium is to develop any real skill, training is required. Some people believe mediumship is an inherited characteristic, but there are many practising mediums who have no family history associated with their ability.

Modern mediumship became especially popular in the early 19th century. Tea party séances were common phenomena, and Spiritualism became a rebellion against Victorian oppression and doctrine. Today's mediums often suffer the same sense of being outcasts as their Victorian ancestors. Although accepted and admired by their clients, unfortunately many are still thought of as frauds or are believed to act as intermediaries for 'the devil'.

Trance Mediumship

Trance mediumship is still popular in many Spiritualist environments. During a self-induced trance state, trance mediums allow spirit entities to take possession of them. This can manifest in things such as a change of voice, using gestures and mannerisms unique to the dead person, and even temporarily taking on the look of the deceased person during a session.

Trance mediumship can feel very odd to the medium. On the few occasions I have allowed myself to go into trance, I feel as though my everyday awareness is put to one side and I become an observer in my own body. The spirit can sometimes reveal itself in the body of the medium. I remember one such occasion vividly. A woman who had lost her husband at a very young age came to see me. When her reading started, I remember feeling the energy of her deceased husband, and then I felt as though it was strongly in me. My awareness began to expand, which for me is a sign of trance mediumship about to begin. The feeling of expanding engulfed my body, almost as though I had become a balloon. Then – the point I remember most vividly as I rushed back into my body – the woman launched herself at me, arms outstretched. Apparently for a few seconds I had become her husband, taking his exact mannerisms, physique and looks. His spirit was utilizing the opportunity to show his wife that he still existed. I know it wasn't a figment of her imagination, because although I have no recollection of the words that were said while her husband took over, she stated that only her husband would know such details.

Personally I prefer to steer away from trance mediumship. Nowadays energy moves much more quickly, and I don't believe a trance is necessary to access decent information during mediumship. I also do not particularly like my awareness to feel separate from my physical being, however briefly. There are, though, plenty of mediums who like the experience and the sensation of trance.

Physical Mediumship

Physical mediumship was popular at the height of late 19th-century Spiritualism. Physical mediumship refers to phenomena such as table tipping, rapping, levitation and materialization. Although sensational, physical mediumship offers little proof of life after death because of the huge potential for fraud. This is why you see little effort nowadays towards this choice of mediumship. During the height of Spiritualism, mediums resorted to magic tricks to create the necessary special effects. In recent times, magicians have used the tricks of Victorian times to demonstrate the possible fraudulent activity of people claiming to be mediums.

Many teenagers have been known to frighten themselves by dabbling in what they expect mediumship to be. They enjoy playing around with makeshift Ouija boards and table tipping, a physical aspect of mediumship where spirits are said to tip the table. On occasion, the effects can be described as aspects of their own psyches creating energy movements rather than any form of spirit assistance. On the few occasions where they have linked with those in spirit, it is my opinion they have linked with earth bound entities who can use the phenomena of physical mediumship easily because they are still on the earth plane. This form of playing around with no one present who has mediumship experience or the correct intention is, in my view, potentially harmful and can startle someone beyond what is necessary.

Mental Mediumship

Mental mediumship is what most of us expect when we think of mediumship. It involves the passing of messages from the other side through clairvoyance (seeing), clairaudience (hearing) and clairsentience (feeling). Mental mediumship offers the strongest evidence of life after death. Mental mediumship will mirror mannerisms and characteristics of the spirit communicators. Mediums will use the words the deceased would have used to describe something, and will offer previously undisclosed information the sitter will recognize. This may be something that is absolutely out of the ordinary, but if the spirit person communicating cannot think of anything particularly revolutionary then the 'proof' will seem very commonplace indeed.

With regard to proving life after death, there are many tests that have been performed by scientists in controlled circumstances. On rare occasions the tests have proven successful, but most mediums have failed to perform to the extent that scientists require as definitive proof.

In my opinion, many of these tests are not representative of the mediumship skill. Like all human beings, mediums are not machines. Natural skills come forth in tune with the sitter. Nerves would also have a profound effect on the results of any sitting. Controlled laboratory experiments will not make for representative or accurate results. It's like having a surprise driving test. Most people who have driven for ages have developed their own habits, good and bad, and if subjected to a test might well fail, even though in normal life they are quite capable drivers. Furthermore, most mediums do not choose their profession. They certainly do not wake up one morning and say, 'Do you know what? I'm going to make a profession out of conning people into thinking dead people talk to me.' The profession chooses them. You may be reading this and struggling with your own calling towards the psychic profession, but most who find themselves caught in the process of reading for people did not choose that path; instead, the path opened up before them.

Certainly for me I went against all the social conditioning of my environment. The original disapproval from my mother was enormous. Believe me, if there had been an easier route I would have taken it. The very person who brought me into this world desperately wanted me to stop pursuing my skill.

Sceptics' View of Mediumship

Sceptics have one or two general views; one is that all of what mediums and psychics are about is mumbo-jumbo and fake, the other is that they have mental health issues. Some argue that many of the phenomena associated with mediumship – such as visions, altered states of consciousness and possession by spirits – are similar to what occurs in certain mental health disorders such as bipolar illness, schizophrenia or multiple personality disorder. Some psychologists and psychiatrists who have investigated prominent mediums have concluded that mediumship is a form of mental disorder and that 'spirits' are secondary personalities of the medium emerging from the unconscious. I myself was approached by a trainee clinical psychologist earlier this year. She asked me to volunteer some 'subjects' for investigation to see if people claiming to have mediumship skills were disturbed by the voices they could perceive. I didn't offer anyone for investigation, and I'm not sure she would have found many mediums willing to participate in her research.

The Spiritualist perspective would argue that any similarities among mediumship and mental health issues are not strong enough to suggest any link. Schizophrenics and people with multiple personality disorder typically have little or no control over the voices, visions and personalities that appear randomly and without warning. They also find the experience disorientating and unproductive, and in most circumstances they find it difficult to incorporate into their everyday lives.

Mediumship, by contrast, is a psychic gift that mediums learn very quickly how to control. They are able to continue with their ordinary daily lives and also to use mediumship for spiritual growth. The communication with spirits is something that does not disturb them, and the messages passed on can be verified.

Certainly I have come across people who have been hearing voices they believe to be spirit but who are in fact mentally ill. The difference between a person who is genuinely suffering from mental health issues and those displaying mediumship skills is, in my opinion, obvious to even the most untrained eye.

Clairvoyance

The word *clairvoyance* derives from the French word meaning 'clear seeing' and refers to the ability to see an event or image in the past, present or future. This form of sight does not happen with your physical eyes but with your 'third eye' chakra, centred in the middle of your forehead on the inside of your skull. Clairvoyant ability means you can receive information in the form of visual symbols or images.

Some clairvoyants would describe the images as a television screen passing through their minds; others would say they receive symbols for interpretation. The way I receive clairvoyant information is a mixture of both. Sometimes I will see what I am to explain, and other times I will receive information distinctly in the form of symbols and metaphors unique to the sitter.

Psychic visions typically appear internally through the mind's eye. Often the images are very clear and are accompanied by feelings and words. In my experience, the visions I have received for a person and his or her future are not unalterable; they can be changed if required. More often than not, in the first instance people do not take action to change or handle certain outcomes as a result of a reading. It is only when they have been forewarned and, therefore, forearmed a couple of times that they then take some or all of the information presented and seek to adjust what they feel necessary to change. I have seen this especially around work scenarios for people. In their readings it may become apparent that it is time to change their jobs. It may then turn out they have wanted to change jobs for a long time but haven't got round to it. I have said that it really is time to change, and such and such an opportunity will come up. They've skipped the opportunity only to find themselves unemployed a few months later. This is not to say all information during a reading should be adhered to, as we all have choices in life. It is merely an opportunity to point out that people do begin to take notice if they know the psychic well, and perhaps haven't previously acted on advice that would have served them well.

It is also my experience that if choices don't come up during clairvoyance, then choices are not particularly part of the equation, so that part of the sitter's life is mapped out no matter what. I have also seen instances where a particular decision has come up simply to allow someone to prepare for a particular outcome, and the energy is apparent that it won't change no matter how much the person tries to force it. When this is the case, I have found the images to be accompanied by feelings that affirm the situation. This has been very common around questions to do with relationships. Often, no matter how much a person wants something to work, however the person tries to 'make' someone love them, the images and feelings show it isn't going to happen – even when fixing it seems possible when the relationship is examined logically.

There are several different types of clairvoyance, including the ability to see auras (auric sight), to see the past (retro-cognition) and to see the future (precognition). Different states of clairvoyance also include the ability to see through objects and into health conditions (body scanning) and to experience visions through dreams (dream clairvoyance). These added abilities within clairvoyance are not necessarily things that act independently of normal clairvoyance but generally as complementary skills.

Often during readings people will ask me to look at their health. When I do this, I do adjust into a slightly different type of clairvoyant skill. I 'see' inside the body and how things are flowing. I am given ways to describe alterations you wouldn't say are medical but that get to the same point. On many occasions I have 'seen' people's blood as 'sticky with bits in', and they have gone to the doctor to discover they need to do something about cholesterol levels.

Now when I see 'sticky' blood I know to suggest a cholesterol test. I have 'looked' at known tumours many times. I see them and receive information on the activity of the tumour. Sometimes the tumour takes on a character or personality for me to interpret. I can then describe my view of its activity. Subsequent tests have shown that although my description wasn't orthodox I have accurately stated what a tumour is up to and whether it is calm (benign) or aggressive (malignant).

Clairvoyance tends to be the strongest in people with high visual skills. If you think in pictures and notice how things look or appear before you take in the rest, then clairvoyance is likely to be your primary channel for processing information.

There are two other psychic arenas to consider, however: clairsentience and clairaudience.

Clairsentience

The word *clairsentience* is again derived from a French word, this time meaning 'clear feeling' or 'clear sensing'. It involves the ability to pick up information through smell, taste, touch, gut feeling and intuition.

Feeling what is around you is the most common way to receive psychic information. All people experience clairsentience through fleeting impressions, but most are either rarely aware of it or they actually ignore it. For example, we are all drawn towards some people more than others for no 'obvious' reason.

Everyone is capable of picking up on emotions through clairsentience to a certain degree. At some point or another we have all felt the 'atmosphere' of a room. We all know when someone is in a bad mood even if they've not said a word. We can feel it. If you are emotional, empathetic and compassionate by nature and you are often affected by the moods of others around you, then it is likely your psychic impressions will primarily come through clairsentience rather than clairvoyance or clairaudience. If you are uncertain, think back to how you learned things at school. If you found it easier to have things shown to you in order to get the feel of how to do them rather than reading something in a book or hearing it from a teacher, then your primary psychic sense is likely to be clairsentience. Strong-feeling people who are 'touch' people will most certainly be clairsentient. In neuro-linguistic programming (NLP) terminology, these people are described as processing information kinaesthetically.

Touch and Non-touch People

'Touch' people are those who like to hug people and touch them. They often stand very close to others and can often intrude into another person's space; they do not particularly notice that it might be uncomfortable for the other person. Extreme touch people will often assume that a 'non-touch' person is unfriendly or stand-offish as they pull away to try and get the extreme touch person out of their space. If you put a group of touch people together, within about ten minutes there will be a bundle of hugs in the middle of the room. It is easy for touch people to feel rejected, since their demonstration of affection comes from being close to people. Sometimes they may have non-touch family or friends. They can feel rejected in this sort of circumstance.

Non-touch people do not like others to touch them unless they know them extremely well. Extreme non-touch people will do everything they can to avoid being hugged, and prefer to feel close to people through conversation and talking about things they have in common. If you put a room full of non-touch people together, they will be in deep conversation about nine feet apart from one another! Extreme non-touch people tend to have clairvoyance as their primary psychic skill.

It is unfortunate that many people may assume they are not loved because of a misunderstanding or different approach to life. For example, perhaps as a touch person you grew up with non-touch parents. As a touch child you would have been very affectionate, needing lots of cuddles, but your non-touch parents' way of showing affection perhaps was to read you a story or help you with your homework. Reacting from their own way of being, rather than seeking to adjust to yours, may have created an unintentional void or misunderstanding. For the budding psychic it is important to adjust to those who are perhaps distinctly different from yourself, rather than perhaps incorrectly assuming they are hostile (touch to non-touch) or in your face (non-touch to touch).

Clairaudience

Clairaudience also comes from the French, meaning 'clear hearing'. It is the ability to hear psychic impressions of sounds, such as music and voices, which are not audible to normal hearing. It is also the ability to hear clear messages within your own psyche through communication with your own higher self, spirit guides and spirits of the deceased. Obviously such communication is not associated with mental health issues, as the communication is often subtle, clear and does not instruct you to do anything harmful. As you would listen to someone talking to you in your everyday life, clairaudience is not any different; the sounds just come on a slightly different frequency to normal.

Besides voices, those with clairaudience may hear other sounds that give them psychic insight. These may include music, whispering, laughter, crying, bells ringing or other sounds. NLP describes people who process information primarily through hearing as 'auditory'.

If you find it difficult to decide whether you are clairvoyant, clairsentient or clairaudient, it is important to remember you may be a mixture of all three. Out of the three, however, there will be a sense that is more dominant than the others. To maximize your potential, it is advisable to develop your primary skill first. If you do this, the rest will follow.

However, if you are strongly clairsentient there is not much point focusing on clairvoyance. Developing clairsentience will be what enhances your psychic senses, and the visual part will become secondary. If you have strong clairvoyance skills, however, clairsentience will be more natural to you and can be developed in tandem. Developing clairsentience will also help the empathetic side of your nature become more prevalent.

CHAPTER 10
When Your Psychic Skills Are All Too Much

Many people ask me about how to control their ability when it's all a bit overwhelming and uncomfortable. Many of us did not ask for the skill to become part of our lives, it just happened. When it is not expected or life circumstances make it something unpleasant, then learning how to settle it down is important.

There is a belief that some people can be 'too open'. This is true for many who are natural psychics, especially mediums. If someone is especially empathetic and strongly clairsentient, they are most likely to find their new-found (or not-so-new-found) ability something they wish they didn't have. Empathy occurs when we feel for others, both their joy and pain. It is possible to develop empathy so strongly that simply by touching someone you can feel or experience the reality of that person. Those who are strongly clairsentient will feel these realities about other people without even touching them.

The problem is that it is more than possible to carry around those thoughts and feelings, and to find them difficult to shake off. For someone who is tremendously sensitive and hugely clairsentient, this is a difficult position. It won't change, it will not go away, and it will only get stronger. However, there are ways to manage it all so that being overwhelmed becomes a thing of the past.

Developing your psychic skills in this instance will actually help. Ignoring the problem will only make it stronger. I have seen many people quite upset by the fact that they are so sensitive to other people's lives. They find it upsetting when they can see an accident or someone dying ahead of time. The fact is this skill will not diminish and they will continue to feel such events, so the best thing to do is understand them and become more comfortable within the self.

When I was first developing, a friend of mine, who is a fantastic spiritual advisor, told me I was so open it was possibly harmful. He told me I was likely to see with my physical eyes spiritual beings, including angels. He said I would find this too much, and I would begin to wonder if I was hallucinating. I have to say that, pleasant as it was, he was right. It was too much. This great man partially closed my energy field, which was the best thing for me until I understood more of what I was getting myself into. It is common at the early stages of opening for a person to find himself with a very open energy field. After a while it will settle down, though.

Sometimes trauma can blow open a person's aura to create the same feeling. However, in this instance an earthbound spirit can find its way into a person's system and try to imprint its life onto the living person. I helped a woman called Hannah who had had such an experience. Hannah's boyfriend's ex-girlfriend had died in an accident. The ex had very low self-esteem in life, and in death she longed to latch onto the energy field of her ex-boyfriend.

Hannah found herself acting in a very similar way to the ex-girlfriend. In life this ex-girlfriend had created the most spectacular dramas in order to feel worthy. Hannah started to have far-fetched dramatic accidents that were completely out of character. Someone at her work then mentioned she could see a woman walking around with Hannah who matched the ex-girlfriend's description. That was when Hannah asked me for help.

I looked into Hannah's energy field and I could see the ex-girlfriend standing there. She was very confused; I would not say she was meaning to be harmful. She said she wanted to be around her ex-boyfriend because he was the man in her life who was safe and secure; he made her feel OK. She had started to imprint her life over Hannah. After the earthbound spirit had said what she wanted, I asked her to leave and pass over properly. Without a fight, once all her feelings were expressed she happily left, never to disturb Hannah or her boyfriend again.

Learning to manage your own emotions means it is much easier to tell the difference between your own and another person's. When you are better able to do this, it is easier to observe the reality of the other person rather than fully experience it in your own body. This does not mean you then become uninterested or hard; it simply means you are better able to detach and view things empathetically rather than having to take over the experience completely. Your psychic skills will then no longer be too much to handle.

CHAPTER 11
Healing

Healing is the channelling of energy for the treatment of illness. Healing may involve touch or the laying-on of hands into the energy field of the person who is ill. Healing can also be given remotely. Some healing is instantaneous, but other 'patients' require numerous treatments.

Religious belief is not essential for healers to be successful at what they do, but many healers have strong religious (or certainly spiritual) beliefs. True healers believe that they themselves do not create the healing but rather facilitate the energy to transform, restore and balance the universal life force permeating all living things. An imbalance or depletion in this life force can be caused by poor diet, lifestyle habits, negative thinking and old stored emotional anchors which can lead to illness and unhappiness.

Many healers are said to be born with special healing powers. In many circumstances this is true, but everyone has the ability to link into healing energy and be effective to a certain degree. Healers generally are drawn towards healing and develop their ability through practice. However, with mastering of the higher frequencies in healing comes a certain amount of sacrifice. Serious commitment and strong internal discipline are necessary. This route is not for everyone, but for some healers there is a tremendous internal push to reach this level.

Faith Healing

In faith healing, the focus of the healing is through God. The healer usually lays hands on the patient and becomes a conduit for divine energy. Belief in faith healing has been something of a focus in various societies throughout history, and is fundamental to Christian healing beliefs and prayer groups directed towards healing energies.

Spiritual Healing

There are various forms of spiritual healing, but the main focus is tapping into the universal energy and directing it for healing through good intention. The healer channels the healing energy through the crown chakra into their hands and forward to the patient through the placing of hands just above the physical energy field. The physical energy field is the part of the aura closest to the physical body. It is the last place within a person's energy field before illness or disease become physical. The healing energy helps to dislodge and release the energy of the disease or illness, and can lessen or relieve completely the patient's pain.

Psychic Healing

Psychic healing is the channelling of healing energies through the psychic field. Different from spiritual healing, psychic healing is often very specific. To do psychic healing the person channelling requires a highly developed psychic ability. With spiritual healing, on the other hand, the healer channels positive energy through good intentions.

Psychic healing is particularly good for emotional matters. If you were to think of a situation that has bothered you in the past or present, a stirring of energy will manifest in the body. This could be butterflies in your stomach, anxiety in your chest or a lump in your throat, as well as many other things. This is the 'energy' of the situation still stored in your system. Psychic healing disperses that energy so the issue or situation no longer bothers you, especially if all layers of that energy can be accessed at once.

On many occasions I have seen things being released from the energy system of a person in quite a dramatic way. Often I have witnessed an instant release where a person has come in really quite distressed and has left feeling much better, with the added benefit of having a strong idea of how to resolve a situation in a way that settles it for all involved. This is because psychic healing has an oral component. The healer will psychically link into the cause of an energy block, and give voice to the cause of the distress. Vocalizing within the patient's energy system helps the patient come to a conscious realization of the energy releasing itself. I have seen people resolve relationship difficulties, health conditions, work problems and stress very quickly using psychic healing.

With psychic healing the healer will look for specific areas within the energy field of the person being treated. These may relate to emotions or physical conditions that need to go through a healing process. The psychic energy is then built to a much higher vibration, so the lower frequencies of the offending energy can be dispersed and released. The psychic healer can interpret the energy being released and relate back to the patient what the build-up was all about, often citing specific episodes or stages in the person's life. The psychic healer will either use a 'hands-on' method to access this information (similar to a spiritual healer), or the more experienced may use remote healing.

While receiving psychic healing a person may feel a variety of emotions and sensations. They may feel heat, they may feel pressure as though someone is pushing down on them, an array of old feelings passing through, or they may see images of past situations that have upset or hurt them. In some instances people feel physical pain for a few seconds as the body goes back into the memory of the offending blocked energy that is being released. Once the process is complete, the person will often feel very relaxed and tranquil, and the situation that previously bothered them will feel as though it is some distance away.

There is plenty of evidence to suggest that the success of healing in both its spiritual and psychic forms works, although the precise reason for this remains unknown. Various laboratory experiments using mice show healers as having the ability to speed up or slow down the growth of cancerous cells through prayer or intense thought projection. There have been many other experiments whose results suggest the merits of healing energies.

Several factors have been suggested as the reasons behind successful healing techniques. First, the presence of large amounts of the universal life force, either strongly present in the healer or in the environment from which they are working. Such places as Lourdes, for instance, burst with the universal life-force energy used for healing. Second, an attitude of openness helps the patient to receive the energy offered. If a person's energy is closed off and, on a deep level, they do not wish to receive healing, no matter the strength of the healer or the quality of the healing energy channelled, the person will not get results. A positive attitude from the patient, whether conscious or unconscious, helps the healer transmit the energy. Finally, a compassionate perspective from the healer helps to access a higher frequency of energy to facilitate a release, together with gratitude for the skill and ability of those involved, whether living (the healer) or in an energetic form (universal energy, angelic or light beings).

The majority of medical views on the subject of healing are sceptical, suggesting the benefits of the craft are 'merely' psychological or can be ascribed to the placebo effect. However, in the UK medical doctors are able to prescribe this form of healing (psychic or spiritual, although usually the term 'faith' healing is preferred), and it is available in some hospitals.

Emotional Healing

Both spiritual and psychic healing can be effective for emotional healing. During the moving of energy to create a circumstance where emotional healing can occur a process takes place. A person will move from sensitivity to acceptance. Where perhaps something was a sensitive issue, they will progress to an understanding and letting go, moving from anger to a place of peace. This is achieved through the manipulation of energy, only it doesn't involve talking or counselling.

Physical Healing

Spiritual healing is traditionally used for physical rather than psychic healing. However, psychic healing is very useful for finding the emotional cause underlying a physical condition. It is my opinion that a person's cells contain emotional memory. Although it may sound strange, during psychic healing those cells communicate during a release. I find that the part of the body hurting will say what has happened to it. On one occasion during a class the whole group witnessed the face of one of the attendees temporarily swell and go black as though bruised during a healing. I was 'pulling' the old energy of an injury from her face and could see in my mind the woman sitting on a bench clutching her face. The injury was 'saying' it hurt from a time she fell over in a park. At that moment she cried out, 'My face, my face, it hurts,' then the bruising appeared temporarily on her face. She said afterwards that yes, indeed, she had tripped and fallen in a park several years previously and still had pain from the incident. I've known her for a number of years since then, and she has never complained of facial pain since the release of energy from this devastating injury.

In order to be successful, the moving of energy for physical healing usually follows a particular process. That process involves the patient accepting an emotional cause as the source of the physical complaint. The healing then helps to create a stress release from the affected area. The stress release involves giving up the physical condition because it no longer serves a purpose. If it is appropriate, and if the physical condition is not serving an emotion any longer, often the patient will experience a release immediately or over the following few days. The 'release' will be an energy movement that the patient might experience as pain relief, reduction in swelling, feeling 'lighter', or as a calm.

The Calling to Become a Healer

For many there is a 'calling' to become a healer, as though it is part of their birthright. Distinct experiences help to define when you are receiving the gifted-healer call. An amazing understanding of others is the primary sense required for those who feel they are strongly drawn to the healing craft. This strong understanding of others is not a learned behaviour but a natural gift, so a curiosity about people and a genuine concern for them are necessary. Most people when asking the question, 'How are you?' rarely mean it. Very few truly listen to the reply because they are busy thinking of what they want to say, looking for a gap in the conversation or for the other person to be quiet or to get away. True healers listen; they 'feel' the answer. They know when something is wrong, and they notice any changes in people's energy field.

Healing does not imply self-sacrifice; it is about engaging wholeheartedly with the energy of a person for the time they are present with you while maintaining healthy boundaries. True healers may take different forms. Some are working as healers while others wander the earth in other professions. However, all healers, at some point or another, find themselves in a professional field related to healing.

The calling comes with a searching. Most healers, in my experience, found themselves looking for something they could not find and eventually stumbled into an aspect of healing. They may start with something more conventional, such as learning a complementary health technique like massage, aromatherapy or reflexology. The fascination rarely stops there as it moves on to 'something else' and eventually embraces many of the healing arts.

Most fantastic healers have a wounded past. They understand people through experience. Their empathy is often the result of a similar challenge they faced themselves, or they have come across the energy before in someone else. Some profound healers have a history of physical illness, emotional crisis or a violent background. All have overcome aspects of their past that enable them to 'know' what it is like for a woman who can't leave her violent husband, or for a depressed person who has suffered continued physical illness for years and is tired of people telling them to pull themselves together. Profound healers can really feel what it's like to be that person. They can feel another's reality and they can tailor their healing capacities specifically to that individual. They work with people who are taking an active role in their own healing, including taking responsibility for the outcome.

A healer's capacity for channelling a clear frequency of universal energy increases as their desires and wishes change. Many find themselves wanting change and embracing it in their everyday existence. Fear becomes secondary, and the healer finds him- or herself wanting progress in life but going through a stage of feeling that life is rather static before an increase in coincidence moves things forward. The increase in coincidence reflects the speedier vibration of the healer.

Self-discipline is vital for the natural healer who is dedicated to the path. Self-discipline involves a mastering of your own mind and the ability to direct the power of the universal energy flow. But this skill should only be used when the healer is absolutely ready to embrace it, having full knowledge of the consequences. After all, you wouldn't give matches to a child to play with. Only when children reach an age when they can understand the consequences of fire would you then expect them to use matches appropriately and without supervision. Healing works in the same way. The more 'mature' the healer becomes, the stronger the level of energy he or she can channel.

Managing the 'ego' is part of self-discipline. Healers engaging with a high level of energy must already have any forms of their own addiction or strong habits under control. They rarely, if ever, engage in 'low-frequency' activities because to do so would alter their effectiveness. Some examples of these low-frequency activities would be an excessive use of alcohol, food, caffeine, tobacco or other prescription or recreational drugs. There are some healers who do still have habits and addictions. It is generally considered they will be in a situation where they are avoiding their own healing or in the process of correcting it. Usually if a healer starts out with any of these habits they will lose interest in poisoning their body, so to speak, because it does not match up with what they do (or seek to do) for others. It is also about congruency: the truest healers match their internal with their external reality by adhering to their truth. Thus, to be really effective, a healer's life must be put together by what he or she really wants rather than allowing any aspects of it to be compromised. A happy healer makes a hugely effective individual.

Necessities of the Healer

When it comes to the potential healer, the saying, 'Physician, heal thyself' is a truly important one. Most people would not like to be treated by a practitioner who does not take care of him- or herself. If you were going to someone to have your energy cleaned, it is likely you would want that person to have clean energy. Such habits as smoking or using alcohol, caffeine or recreational drugs do not result in a healthy energy field.

If your desire is to be a successful healer, something beyond mere dabbling, and particularly if you wish to help people overcome quite serious challenges, then there are some pointers to consider.

Those particularly interested in psychic healing require a discipline beyond what is expected from spiritual healing. This is because psychic healing requires a high level of psychic ability or the willingness to develop fully this part of the self. In order to access a high frequency of energy and sustain it, healing requires you to work consciously on yourself in terms of understanding some of your own unconscious traits. Healers must cleanse themselves of negative emotional baggage in order for their energy to pass through. The quality of the energy is then high and is more likely to assist others.

Physician, Heal Thyself

No one is perfect! Even the most capable healer will continue to create blocks of one sort or another. We continue to create blocks along the way because at some point or another we all see life as unsafe. We block in patterns that involve our whole energy system. Our energy system is designed to protect us against invading energies, and we are not supposed to hold on to that energy. For the healer, it is important to maintain a flow. If the healer is bothered by something or someone, they should question and deal with their feelings and their feelings only.

Acknowledge, Process, Let Go

Acknowledge to yourself that you are bothered by someone/ something.

Process those feelings through self-examination. Examine your response to that situation or person. What did they trigger in you?

Let go. Forgive yourself and thank the person or situation in your life for having shown you what you needed to sort out within yourself.

When Healing Doesn't Work

No matter the capabilities of a healer, a person will only heal to the extent he or she is willing to let go. If a person is stubbornly holding on to an old belief, let them. Very experienced healers learn their own techniques to shift stubborn energy, but sometimes it will not shift. This is because the person holding on to it is not ready to let go. They have not yet learned the lesson the energy was created for. If the healer pursues with an energy that is not ready to shift, he or she will tire unnecessarily.

In my experience, healing will not work for a physical condition that is too entrenched in the system when there is not much time left. This is true in cases where there is tremendous emotional history to unlock and not much time to do it. I have seen this in instances of terminal illness where the person has tried every other method, healing being the last resort.

The story of a woman I met a few years ago comes to mind. In her early thirties, she had been diagnosed with terminal cervical cancer and had been told she had six months to live. Defiant, she told me she did not believe it and was prepared to do whatever was necessary to keep living. She had a young son she was desperate not to leave behind.

As she sat in front of me while she told me her story, I began to scan her energy field. The tumour was shown to me as a huge lump that resembled a piece of root ginger. The root had 'tentacles' and lots of them. To me, that symbolizes a fast-growing cancer, which I saw as three months of her life left, not six. I did not pass this on to the woman; I sat quietly listening to her story.

When it was my turn to speak, I told her the energy of her cancer revealed that the reason for its presence had to do with a sibling rivalry between herself and her younger sister. She looked at me blankly, stating she had no rivalry with her sister. I explained I could only read what the energy stated. With that, a tirade came out of her mouth about her relationship with her sister. The years of anger and resentment poured from her lips. After 15 minutes or so had passed she finally stopped. She looked at me, stunned, and said 'I really don't know where that came from.'

That was the last time I saw her, for there was no time available to do all the emotional work that was needed for the cancer to loosen its grip. There was also the fact that, as with so many with terminal illnesses, she did not want to acknowledge there was any need for haste. Her husband called me and left a message. She had died the day before, almost three months to the day since I had seen her.

Over the years I have dealt with several cases of terminal illness. Some have healed and some have died. I have noticed a clear pattern in these situations. The ones who died did not come for healing in order to live; their soul energy came for peace and understanding. In each case I saw it as a fleeting flash across their eyes; had I just blinked I would have missed it.

CHAPTER 12
Psychic Children

Children regularly send me emails asking questions about managing their psychic skills. Many of these children send the emails without the knowledge of their parents. Similar to my experience, these children are often unsupported or misunderstood by their parents when all they are trying to do is make sense of something. The children who have contacted me write so clearly and concisely and in such a very adult manner that I often wonder if they are mini-Einsteins.

The queries I receive come from children all over the world. They are usually between ten and 16 years old, and many are boys. They tell me about all the amazing things they can do, such as seeing future events in the lives of their loved ones or hearing communications from their dead relatives. Often they only want to ask me if their experiences are real, because so many around them either refuse to believe them or are frightened by what they say.

These children are truly gifted. Even without much knowledge of their lives I can tell they are extremely intelligent, well above average. Their sense of direction in life is incredible, and their maturity and wisdom are well ahead of those of the average human being. The children developing today will become profound psychics, and there are many of them. I believe intuition and psychic ability in years to come will be part of our mainstream intelligence. The pathway has been opened by what are now known as 'the Indigo Children'.

Indigo Children

During the latter part of the 1970s, Nancy Ann Tappe, a psychic and lecturer at the University of San Diego in California, noticed a change taking place in the colour of children's auras. Nancy believed her ability to see an aura was due to her synesthesia (a condition where two neurological pathways cross so the senses get reversed – for example, when the hearing of a certain sound induces the visualization of a certain colour).

Indigo being the colour of the third eye chakra, Nancy concluded that many of these 'Indigo children' were clairvoyant. She believed the Indigo children came into this world as 'rebels with a cause' and were here to raise the vibration of the planet. They have a warrior nature, and adults find their intense energy difficult to handle. Often mis-labelled as ADHD (Attention Deficit Hyperactivity Disorder), many found their formative years dulled down with prescription drugs. Nancy Tappe suggested that actually these children have right- and left-brain alignment, something people on the spiritual path strive for throughout their lifetimes. They are highly sensitive, they have powerful psychic abilities and they possess incredible wisdom.

According to Lee Carroll Kyron, who has written a great deal about Indigo children, the typical signs of an Indigo child are said to be:

- They come into the world with a sense of royalty and feel strongly that they deserve to be here.
- They come into the world with their self-worth intact.

- They have difficulty with authority when it is presented without choice. They will not be 'told' what to do, but they will respond to being 'asked'.

- They get frustrated with systems that are rule-orientated and either don't require or actively discourage creative thought.

- They can see better ways of doing something, so are often seen as nonconformists.

- They don't respond to 'guilt' discipline.

- They are not shy in letting you know what they need.

Star and Crystal Children

Indigos paved the way for the next wave of gifted children. These are now known as 'Star' and 'Crystal' children. These are the young children with whom I believe I have found myself corresponding recently. They are gentler by nature than the Indigo children and have come into this world certainly with a strong sense of self, regardless of their circumstances. They are highly intelligent and do not show the signs of what has previously been labelled ADHD in Indigos. They are much softer by nature, and they communicate by negotiation rather than force. Way ahead of their years, they have an extraordinary wisdom I have not seen before.

These children know they have a birthright to change something fundamental in the world. They ask me questions of how to handle their extraordinary psychic gifts in a world that still doesn't understand them. They don't need to be heard; they simply want to know what to do while their skills are maturing. They are not gung-ho, but have a pragmatic approach. If you have one of these children, you'll know.

I tell most of them the same thing, as they ask me the same questions: 'What shall I do?', 'Does everyone see?' They are not fearful children, but they *are* very sensitive. They find violence a disturbing and brutally primitive act. I tell them to focus on learning about life and how to understand its complexities. I tell them to enjoy themselves and to have as many experiences as they can so they understand life first-hand. I tell them to put their psychic skills to one side for now; the true sense of their ability will form later. There will be plenty of time for them to fulfil what it is they are here to do, as sometimes they can be a little too responsible for their own good!

I tell them their psychic senses will get stronger as each year goes by. It is hugely important for these children to steer clear of drugs and alcohol because their 'electrical' charges are so high. I have noticed, though, that these children naturally find themselves far away from possible influences that could steer them in that direction.

When distressed, these children can create havoc. Their energy fields start firing in all directions, and they can easily start activity in the house you might otherwise think is being caused by a poltergeist. They do not do this intentionally; it is their thought patterns and energy fields creating the psychic disturbances. I know of one such child. Distressed by his parents' divorce, he went around triggering old gramophones to start playing music and caused ChapSticks to appear standing up in the middle of the living room even though he hadn't been near either item. Once his energy was evened out and calmed down, all the activity stopped.

These children love healing and respond extremely well to it. If you have one of these children you may notice that they love meditation and relaxing ways to balance their energy systems. They are not particularly into contact sports – they like harmony and music. When they are babies, you will find they respond very well to classical music and get disturbed by any sort of loud noises or thumping music. As toddlers they eat only what they need. They will not overeat and they love plain foods. They are great at creative play and will happily play alone. They have friends but no major attachments, preferring to have a few good friends rather than many acquaintances. They speak when they need to, and words they don't need they won't use. They are absolutely fantastic at telepathic communication. If they have a telepathic rapport with someone, conversation is minimal but perfectly comfortable.

CHAPTER 13
Top Ten Tips for Psychic Development

When I first started to develop my psychic skills I was living at home with my parents. At first I was very angry with the dismissive attitude of my parents, especially my mother. She had always been very supportive of my other interests, including the horses that we kept and the show-jumping events every Sunday morning. But this was different. She completely refused to support my 'spooky' stuff.

Similar to many people I have come across over the years, the compulsion to discover more about the sixth sense did not wane, it only got stronger. Unfortunately, as it got stronger I had to become more secretive. I explored many avenues through workshops and books before I accepted that psychic and healing work was something I was interested in.

Most of us are attracted to psychic growth more through curiosity about our own potential than by any deep-seated desire to become a practising medium or psychic. Whatever your desire, here are some pointers that will accelerate your psychic growth.

1 Meditation and Inner Work

We are all very used to living in the physical world, and exploring and understanding the inner world is alien to most people. Meditation is considered boring by many people, and inner work is avoided because of the skeletons it uncovers. However, both are vital for psychic development.

The ego in its traditional sense is a tool of the physical world. It is necessary for the basics of survival, but beyond that it has major limitations. In the psychic realms it becomes too dense and soon becomes an obstacle. The lessening of your familiar identity is a major means of psychic success. Meditation and inner work enable you to become more aware of the wonders of the energies of the universe. These practices enable you to link with the deepest part of your inner self while opening your awareness to the ebb and flow of the energetic frequencies unavailable to the ego self.

When I first started to develop my psychic skills, I would lie in bed at night, close my eyes and start to observe my thoughts. In the end my brain would relax, and eventually I would still be conscious but in a deepened state in which I could see an array of amazing colours and experience a pulsating feeling across my eyes. It was worth the wait. At first your attempts at this may be frustrating, as you keep falling asleep, but with persistence you'll find you remain alert and your mind begins to open up. It came to a point when I would see going to bed as the greatest part of the day because of the amazing things I became more aware of.

I used short, guided meditations in order to open up my visual skills. A lot of people believe they are 'no good at visualizing', but for many people it just takes practice. Certainly those who have done meditation before find it easy to sink into the different experiences created by the class environment. I'm a firm believer in the idea that our conscious mind can hold information for about ten minutes, at best, before we mentally 'wander off'. Even today, the mediations I provide for classes and my CDs is kept under 20 minutes, usually about ten, so that people gain the full experience rather than fall asleep halfway through. Saying that, guided meditations are a good way to help you fall asleep. Listening to them helps to relax the brain. If you're relaxed, good-quality sleep is likely.

My husband describes trying to wake me as more difficult than 'waking the dead'. He will often ask if I heard our son jumping around at 2 a.m. Usually I have no clue what he's talking about. I am able to sleep so deeply because my mind is trained to be quiet. I have done this simply through the discipline of meditation and inner work.

2 Nutrition

In terms of psychic skills, the saying, 'You are what you eat' is true. It is known the world over that what you eat affects your behaviour. There are children who have had learning difficulties and behavioural issues corrected with nutrition, and it is true of adults also. As with everything else, one's diet should reflect moderation; but if you switch to a mainly nutritious diet full of fresh foods, you will find your mind opens and flourishes very quickly. I am not suggesting you eat carrots and lettuce for the rest of your days in order to be psychic, but 'calm' foods do help the psyche rest and relax. A relaxed mind is perfect for psychic and intuitive skills to become evident.

Personally, I used to eat a lot of cream cakes, cheese and milk. I really found my psychic skills flourished when I developed a sensitivity to these foods. They were cut out of my life for a period of a few years. Now I have little interest in any of them, and I only use goat's milk now. I do love chocolate and still eat quite a bit of it, but I buy good-quality chocolate because I'm conscious of what I put into my body. I truly believe that over the years I have developed intolerances to most toxic substances in food because of the sensitivity of the work I do. E numbers and additives are a no-go area, and generally tend to be so for psychics.

Some people believe that in order to be psychic you have to eat a vegetarian diet. I can't say I completely agree with this. I believe some people need meat because their bodies can't assimilate essential proteins any other way. Perhaps they don't need it every day, but just often enough for iron levels and other vitamins and minerals to maintain the body. I eat meat, and I have found it actually enhances my psychic skills, not diminishes them. I was vegetarian for a while, but during that time I was constantly tired. I find meat and carbohydrates to be positively grounding.

3 Imagination

Nowadays we all know that imagination is important for child development. There are 'stimulation toys' and 'development aids' in every major supermarket and toy shop. Imagination remains important well into your adult years as well. Imagination helps the psyche to experience pleasure beyond external stimuli, as it creates opportunities for 'thinking' our way out of difficulties and enables our minds to think more quickly. These are all crucial parts to effective and long-term psychic skills, especially with regard to the self and other people.

If your imagination is 'open', then you are better able to allow the psychic side of your nature to strengthen. Imagination draws energy in for interpretation and gives access to areas that otherwise remain static and within the limitations of the ego. Stimulating the imagination and improving it is easy. For some, it may take time. One of the fundamental – though controversial – ways is to switch the TV off for a month and to stay away from computer games. This is especially important if you struggle using your imagination! These two things, television and computer games, do the imaginative work for you; they are external stimuli and make your own imagination lazy.

Furthermore, if you haven't already got a deck of Tarot cards, then get some to use for stimulating your imagination. Look at the images and 'imagine' what they mean. Let the cards talk to you, and read up on the mythology around them. Pause to think about their meaning. Persistence pays off, and this is a guaranteed way to stimulate your imagination.

Join a creative writing course at your local adult-education centre. This may seem ridiculous to some, but you'd be surprised how much it will stimulate your imagination and open it up. Those who have a fabulous imagination live a happy life, for they are never bored. Their creative thoughts generate ideas to solve problems, and issues in life flow without effort. Think how children with vivid imaginative skills can play for hours, while those who have neglected these skills get bored very quickly and need ever-changing sources of amusement.

When I first started to develop my psychic skills, I would go out to ride my horse or to walk the dog. I would look at the tree lines and let myself imagine what it would be like to see the auras of the wildlife (which a book I'd been reading said it was possible to do). I would imagine understanding something new or working out how to fix something that wasn't going the way I wanted it to. After a while I found myself looking at the wondrous, colourful energy fields of trees and plants and somehow knowing the thoughts and feelings of my horse and dog. I knew the dog was sick, as he 'told me' long before he died. My horse would 'talk' by being silly but always safe. As we grew to trust each other and enjoy play time together, my imaginative skills developed tremendously!

4 Reading

In my experience, one of the best ways to develop your psychic skills is to read. Read all the material that you find interesting and you will quickly become comfortable with the possibility of your psychic skills. Knowledge dissolves fear. If you have found your psychic and intuitive skills increasing without your choosing, then it is likely you will find this frightening. Reading helps you understand and therefore to feel more comfortable and relaxed. It also helps you to explain to yourself psychic phenomena that could otherwise be disconcerting.

When I first started, I read every book going. At first I read mostly on psychology because I thought that was what I was interested in. When I found my first psychic-development book I was ecstatic! I finally began to understand what on earth had been happening to me over the years. I read that book over and over again. I had no idea at the time where to find such material, but now there is much more like it everywhere. Whole sections of bookshops are dedicated to the mystic arts and self-development, so you have plenty to choose from.

5 Patience

Those with no real outcome in mind but who have a fascination with psychic development are the most promising psychics. The greatest thing you are up against when developing psychic skills is impatience. Your interest may have been aroused because of a psychic experience or a fascination with the ability to 'read' people. You can't really blame yourself for wanting to get on with it. However, with great ability comes great responsibility. If any parts of the full picture are skipped, psychic skills will be surface-level only, and ultimately meaningless.

Essentially, everyone has a different way of experiencing psychic ability. There are no fixed ways, but being patient and exploring all avenues before declaring yourself an expert will give you a fantastic and wholesome approach. Psychic skills are not a destination, they are part of a journey of discovery to be enjoyed.

Lots of people in classes and workshops say to me, 'How can you do that? I'm never going to be able to do that!' Perhaps you won't; perhaps you will. My psychic skills are not perfect; they are *a* way of looking at something, not *the* way. Patience helps you to master your strengths and be aware of your weaknesses. When learning anything, I like to learn it properly. I don't mind if it takes a while, as the technique is important to me. Skiing is one of my interests; it has taken me years to ski properly. I've had lots of lessons because I want to ski properly, safely and in control, not only for my own sake but for the safety of others on the slopes. I have been able to 'get down' a slope for a long time, but mastering it, doing it properly, is part of my enjoyment. It is also how I developed my psychic skills. Patience pays off.

6 Feet on the Ground

We live in a world where it is necessary to provide a roof over our heads, food on the table and clothes on our back. Therefore, it is a requirement in the real world to have our feet firmly on the ground. Unfortunately, many people interested in the spiritual realm struggle to keep themselves fully present in the real world. They struggle to accept that money is part of the exchange system, an energy used to reflect giving and taking. They are uncomfortable with anything more than basic requirements, and find providing for themselves a challenge. Quite a few have idealistic aspirations rather than realistic ones. Generally they find it difficult to keep their attention on practical necessities.

153

Focusing on keeping grounded means that any ability you develop within the psychic realms is real. Grounded people can discern very well information they receive through their psychic channels. The challenge we all face at some point or another is whether something is real or imagined, logical or psychic. Those with strong psychic ability and their feet on the ground are the most powerful and accurate psychics available. Those with strong psychic skills but with their heads in the clouds become average-to-weak psychics over a period of time. This is because discerning what is useful within the real world becomes misty for them.

Grounding is easy and difficult all at the same time! To be very grounded you have to be comfortable in your own body, fully present in the 'now' and comfortable with your existence in the physical world. Most spiritual people at some stage go through the feeling they are not sure they belong in the world; they feel separate from it. They can feel they 'belong' somewhere else, and it is not easy to define where 'home' is. This is when you remember that you came from the perfect place of serenity, harmony and peace. The longing to 'go home' can be painful. This pain subsides as the personality continues to merge with the soul energy, and then suddenly we become very comfortable with life here in the physical body. This is the ultimate state of being grounded.

On an everyday basis, grounding is achieved by stabilizing your energy field. When your energy field is woolly and needs grounding, you feel light-headed and vague. Grounding is easy; it is achieved through the simple act of imagining roots coming from your feet and penetrating deep into the earth. Instantly, the feeling of being more present is achieved with a clearer head.

7 Daydreaming / Quiet Time

Daydreaming and quiet time are essential routes for accelerated psychic and spiritual development. Daydreaming helps the brain to relax and open up to a deeper part of the self. It takes the pressure off what perhaps is already an overloaded system. I love daydreaming and quiet time. I'm so used to it that I now know when I desperately need it. My daydreaming will be staring out of the window at the garden, watching a bee collect pollen or a squirrel busily collecting nuts. If given the opportunity, I could do that for hours.

There is a famous Buddhist saying, 'Before enlightenment, chop wood, carry water; after enlightenment, chop wood, carry water.' Thus, enlightenment does not change your outer world drastically but transforms your inner world to take pleasure in the smallest of things. In the early days, either of those things I would have considered boring and wouldn't have been able to wait to get back to being busy. This is indicative of an overactive, out-of-control mind. Daydreaming helps the mind to become disciplined and focused, giving creativity and psychic inspiration the chance to flood through. Having some quiet time, even five minutes a day, will accelerate your psychic skills. This is because the mind has a chance to decipher what it wants to keep and what parts are surplus to requirements.

There is a free download of my relaxation meditation from my website (see Recommended Resources). If you listen to that for 20 nights before you go to sleep, you will start to experience the 'library' effect. You will have a quiet mind.

8 Exercise – Yoga

Exercise such as yoga will help any form of spiritual development, as spiritual development is essentially the whole point of yoga. Yoga fires up your energy system, keeping it in flow. A lack of exercise for those with a mass of psychic energy pounding through their bodies will result in stagnating energies, irritability and high stress levels. This will often show externally as the constant popping of light bulbs, and your having to replace them every five minutes! Or it will show as electrical items going haywire. This is not directly because you're not exercising but because your energy flow has got a little stuck and your stress levels are building without an active outlet. This also happens when you are first developing your psychic skills, as the rise in frequency or vibration means the energy builds up and struggles initially to find its way out. After a short while the energy settles down again. Those who initially find an interest in yoga often then find their curiosity extends into the inner self and sixth sense. This is because through yoga they have begun to gain access to a whole new area of the self. I have noticed over the years that those attending my classes who are also avid yoga-class attendees often develop in a stronger, more defined way than those who have no interest in the art.

9 Notice

Taking the time to notice the world around you will increase your ability to link with the sixth sense and will train you to use your instinctual capabilities better. This is because the psychic arts are all about noticing often tiny energy changes and impressions in order to define what something means. Noticing your environment increases clairsentient skills very quickly, thus confidence in your intuition increases tenfold.

10 Use Psychic Powers to Learn about Yourself before Using Them for Others

The main purpose in developing your psychic ability should be to learn about *yourself*. You may have had psychic experiences that initially triggered your interest, but the main reason for exploring this area should be you.

People ask me during courses if they should continue because they're not sure they are 'good enough', or they say, 'So-and-so is better than I am.' The question I always ask them is, 'Are you enjoying yourself?' I have always had the answer, 'Yes, of course. I love it!' My answer to that is, 'Then, yes, you very much should be here. As long as you are enjoying yourself, then you are welcome and this is for you.' Over the years I have seen these people flourish and develop their lives tremendously. Sure, they've developed strong psychic skills along the way, but the most amazing thing is they have become a bigger, brighter, happier person by making the journey.

CHAPTER 14
Why My Mother Didn't Want Me to Be Psychic

Now that I am a mother myself, it has become obvious to me why my mother panicked at having a psychic for a daughter. It is only now that I understand the protective instinct of a parent. At times, though, this instinct can show itself as an overbearing attitude of enforced control and opinion.

For two years from the moment I chose to pursue my current life, I had no contact with my immediate family. This happened in my early twenties. Strong disapproval prevailed; my parents lectured me on the perils of the 'cult' I was joining. I have no idea to this day what 'cult' they thought I was joining, but this was a time when having psychic skills was an extremely taboo subject. Nowadays it still is taboo, but slightly more accepted. Still, the stereotypical view of a woman with long fingernails and far too much make-up, with a scarf wrapped around her head and gazing into a crystal ball, still exists in the minds of many when they think of a psychic.

I remember the main concern of my mother when I entered the world of psychic development. She thought I was tampering with something that shouldn't be tampered with. Her wish to avoid looking at what interested me – but which did not fit in with the normal, conventional path – is the same route many parents take when acting in what they see as the best interests of their offspring. She worried I wasn't pursuing a 'normal' job, fitting in with what everyone else's daughters did. What would people think? In her mind, having a daughter who was a psychic meant I would hook a caravan to the back of my car every time the travelling fair moved on.

In truth, she was frightened of losing her daughter to what she imagined was a weird world full of people with their heads in the clouds and performing Druid ceremonies. Her protected world never imagined that Druid ceremonies worshipping the earth could be wholesome and fun. Now I can't say that I've ever been to any Druid ceremonies, but I have taken the trouble to ask those who have. Out of curiosity I have asked many people many questions about how they choose to live their lives, trying always to understand and never to judge until I have the full picture.

Sometimes my husband says, 'You can't ask that!' 'Why not?' I answer. 'I'm interested in finding out why people do what they do.' It has helped me to understand the motivations of people and the reasons they do things that are not always approved of in our society. I have found this curiosity of mine has made my ability to provide a service for people more efficient. I find it easy to link into the whys when someone is hurting over the end of a relationship. I can link into the thoughts of the other person and explain from a neutral standpoint *why* the other person has moved on rather than just telling them they have to accept it.

Perhaps wars would be fewer, misunderstandings corrected and the earth still able to flourish and protect itself if Druid worship were a prominent practice, for the basis of it is to respect Mother Nature! Perhaps then we wouldn't be taking the earth's resources for granted. But that's another subject.

Mums Are Meant to Know Everything

I remember as a child believing my mum had magical powers to know the right thing in every situation. Into our adult years, we still believe our mothers to be right. Perhaps yours told you how great you are, or perhaps yours told you how irresponsible and useless you are, or perhaps yours was neglectful. Whatever the story, we still believe at a deep level whatever our mum told us.

So I believed for a while she was right; perhaps I was entering a world I shouldn't touch, perhaps I should be as conventional as possible. But a deep part of me was emerging, something I had no real control over. It was a soulful understanding operating from a core part of myself. Of course I questioned it, but I never stopped it, for I began to realize it was something bigger than myself. Yes, of course, like most psychics and healers I still wonder what it would be like to live a life directed by what would have made my parents or society in general happy. Over the years I have come to realize few professions are so scrutinized and ridiculed as the psychic arena. I'm not aware of accountants who have to prove their ability to add up every time they meet someone, yet psychics have to deal with the 'Are you fake?' question or the 'Tell me what colour knickers I'm wearing' scenario at some point or another.

Friends at the time took on a similar view as my parents. 'Heidi has become some freak who wants to work as a psychic.' We all have friends like that, and those are the ones to whom we don't mention the deeper parts of our lives for fear of ridicule. Perhaps the deeper part is made up of those beliefs or interests that sit slightly on the edge of what society can cope with. I have heard many participants at workshops keep their interests even from their partners. 'Oh, he wouldn't understand. He thinks I'm at a Tupperware party.'

Then we have the friends who accept and understand us no matter what our choices are. Those are our real friends. I try my best to be one of those, as I understand what it feels like to be on the periphery of what's acceptable and easily judged. Countless times I have been visited by a pair of friends for a reading, or they have come to a workshop together. Why? One has mentioned to the other her interest, and the other has come for moral support. When I went through my most difficult time with friends and family, I had one friend who remained close and loyal, even though he didn't necessarily understand my interests. That friend is still dear to me today, as we have known each other since the age of 12, and I believe he and his wife will remain dear friends with my husband and me until the day we drop off the planet.

People have always considered me 'different', even from an early age. I see my 'difference' as a fascination with seeing the truth. I have always had a keen eye for when someone is lying. I remember at school, even in my eight-year-old naiveté, knowing the priest was always drunk and the nun who walloped her class for asking a question must be unhappy, or that the teacher who asked the girls to sit on his lap for a kiss wasn't right. I would question it in my head for fear of being scolded, which I often was.

That 'difference' has followed me into my adult years, often getting me into trouble for daring to mention a truth. I remember the polite responses I received when first meeting my husband's family. He, in his usual fashion, has always been proud of my capabilities and insists on mentioning them to anyone who will listen. To this day I can remember the look on his mother's face when he introduced me and stated my occupation. His father looked away. His aunt made herself busy, and my occupation was never mentioned again, certainly never to their friends.

My mother wanted me to get a good job and settle down. I'm sure that's what most mothers want for their children. To operate outside the norm is impossible for many to accept. There are people who hide such things as their sexuality or choice of partner from their friends and family for fear of being expelled from the family unit. Sadly, this is very real for some. Through fear they regard it as a secret they must keep for the rest of their lives. What pressure this creates! I am sure such fear contributes to the start of illness and disease in some people.

As a result of my mother's attitude I have learned many things. One is that we may think people try to contain us deliberately, but the truth is they do it from what they perceive as a position of love. I have learned that bitterness never works, no matter how upset I get at the things others do. I have learned how to find determination and a strong desire to be persistent, and I know what is important to me and what I want from life. This has made me a psychic with a wide experience and knowledge of the challenges in life. I can help people from experience. I know that people are comfortable because I can feel what it's like to be in their shoes. I have no fear of people's emotions.

I have learned I have a genuine love for people. I love to see them progress, and I champion their every climb to become stronger, more confident individuals who act by what is true in life. I have learned that I love what I do, and I do what I love. I have learned that balance in life is vital for health and well-being. I have learned that confidence is not an external thing, based on the clothes you wear, your body shape, make-up or cosmetic surgery, but essentially a state of being. It cannot be bought, only developed. I have learned that the classes I teach help people to become strong, internally confident and calm. I would never have had the chance to become aware of all these things if life had been a bowl of cherries. I have learned that difficulties are a challenge, an opportunity to progress. The hardest events in my life are the ones, in hindsight, that I have learned the most from. This is generally the truth for everyone, if only they would let themselves see it this way.

Our outer world is a mirror of our inner reality. This is difficult for many to understand, as generally we would say, 'I didn't ask for that!' But the truth is, a part of us did. Not as a punishment but as a point of learning. Perhaps a part of us either believed we deserved it or it was part of our pre-planned, chosen destiny. Holding pain is painful! It's hard work. This is not to say that people should be forgiven for unacceptable behaviour, but I have learned that if you forgive yourself, then the pressure of keeping things bitter diminishes. I have learned you can help people to see a way through difficulty that is right by all.

Letting go has always been a challenge for my mother. Even recently, letting go of an old car that she never cleaned and that smelt of a hamster cage was difficult. She had many memories tied up in that smelly old Land Rover. So, letting go of her daughter to pursue her passions in life was never going to be easy. It still isn't easy for her, but now she accepts it. She may not agree with my choice of profession, but she accepts the choices I have made. She knows there are a lot of people happy with what I do through the classes I teach and the course materials I sell. She sees the positive feedback, and though she will never understand the nature of my work, she is finally close to understanding me!

AFTERWORD
In Aid of the Scleroderma Society

Ten per cent of all profits from this book will go to the Scleroderma Society.

The society contributes towards research into scleroderma and provides support for patients with the disease.

Scleroderma is an incurable, autoimmune connective tissue disease. The cause is largely unknown, and although there is no cure there are many treatments to slow down the disease's progress. In its worst form, scleroderma will deposit collagen into the major organs of the body, eventually causing them to fail.

The aims of the society are to offer support to patients, who often feel isolated, to increase awareness of the disease and to raise money for vital research. Scleroderma can affect anyone at any age. The majority of sufferers are women.

BIOGRAPHY OF PROFESSOR JOBST

Kim A. Jobst is a physician with a lifelong interest in healing and holistic healthcare. His career began in Agricultural Sciences and Forestry at Oxford University before he completed his degree in Physiological Sciences and Medicine at Oxford. He went on to become fully accredited in Internal Medicine and Homeopathy through the University Department of Medicine in Glasgow, as well as in Neuro-degenerative Diseases and Dementia.

As Clinical Director of The Oxford Project to Investigate Memory and Ageing (OPTIMA) at Oxford University (1988–96), he and his colleagues made fundamental discoveries about the underlying processes, diagnosis, prognosis and therapeutics of the dementias.

Kim trained in traditional Chinese acupuncture, homeopathy and Jungian analytical psychology and has interests in psychosomatic medicine and the meaning of disease in health, wellbeing and healing.

Currently he is Healthcare Advisor to the Bulmer Foundation Charity in Hereford (www.bulmerfoundation.org.uk), Editor-in-Chief of the peer-reviewed scientific *Journal of Alternative and Complementary Medicine: Research on Paradigm, Practice and Policy* (www.liebertpub.com/acm), Visiting Professor in Healthcare and Integrated Medicine at Oxford Brookes University, and serves on a number of scientific advisory boards for emerging energy medicine technologies (e.g., the NeuroResource Group in Dallas, Texas, www.nrg-unlimited.com), Clarus Transphase Scientific in California (www.clarus.com) and the Soukya Holistic Health and Healing Centre in India (www.soukya.com). Dr Jobst runs his own consultancy (Functional Shift Consulting Ltd) and clinical practice in London and Hereford. He has over 100 publications in peer-reviewed journals and is a frequently-invited speaker and workshop/seminar facilitator.

Kim was a founding member of the Council of His Royal Highness The Prince of Wales's Foundation for Integrated Health, and served on the steering group from 1995–2004.

Kim and his wife Belinda live with their daughter and three sons in Herefordshire, England.

Recommended Resources

Professor Kim A. Jobst, MA, DM, MRCP, MFHom, DipAc

Consultant Physician and Medical Homeopath in Integrative Medicine and Healthcare and in Jungian Analytical Psychology and Healing

Specialist in Neuro-degeneration and Dementia

Visiting Professor in Healthcare and Integrated Medicine, Oxford Brookes University

Editor-in-Chief, *Journal of Alternative and Complementary Medicine: Research on Paradigm, Practice and Policy*

Health Advisor, The Bulmer Foundation, Hereford.

Director, Functional Shift Consulting Ltd

Correspondence
Broom House
5 Jasmine Lane
St Mary's Park
Burghill
Hereford
Herefordshire HR4 7QS
UK

tel: (+44) (0)1432 761340 fax: (+44) (0)1432 761463
e-mail: admin@functionalshiftconsulting.com

Clinics
The Diagnostic Clinic
50 New Cavendish St
London W1G 8TL
www.thediagnosticclinic.com

Wye Valley and Glasgow Nuffield Hospitals
http://www.nuffieldhospitals.org.uk

Honorary Consultant Physician, Royal London Homeopathic
Hospital
http://www.rlhh.org.uk/

*Journal of Alternative and Complementary Medicine: Research on
Paradigm, Practice and Policy*, see: www.liebertpub.com/acm
For the work of *The Bulmer Foundation*, see: www.
bulmerfoundation.org.uk

Heidi Sawyer
www.PsychicCourses.com

www.HeidiSawyer.com

Free forum, meditation downloads, articles, monthly newsletter
and online psychic ability test; information on Heidi's courses,
readings, mail-order materials and global psychic circle.